MISSION OF THE
UNIVERSITY

INTERNATIONAL LIBRARY OF SOCIOLOGY
AND SOCIAL RECONSTRUCTION

Editor: Dr. Karl Mannheim

MISSION OF THE UNIVERSITY

by

JOSÉ ORTEGA Y GASSET

TRANSLATED WITH AN INTRODUCTION BY

HOWARD LEE NOSTRAND

LONDON

KEGAN PAUL, TRENCH, TRUBNER & CO., LTD.

BROADWAY HOUSE : 68–74 CARTER LANE, E.C.4

First published in England 1946

THIS BOOK IS PRODUCED
IN COMPLETE CONFORMITY WITH
THE AUTHORIZED ECONOMY STANDARDS

Printed in Great Britain by Butler & Tanner Ltd., Frome and London

CONTENTS

INTRODUCTION

If we could solve the problem of general education, we could confidently strike any third world war off the calendar. General education means the whole development of an individual, apart from his occupational training. It includes the civilizing of his life purposes, the refining of his emotional reactions, and the maturing of his understanding about the nature of things according to the best knowledge of our time.

In this sense general education is the fundamental problem of modern society. Other problems must of course be solved too, before we can achieve the good society which now clearly lies within the reach of man's imagination. Among the others are the problems of international organization and democratic control, the problems of economic co-operation and the freedom of the individual. But we are going to be able to carry out our best plans for all these things, in the years ahead, *only so far as they are understood and supported by the people* of many countries, particularly countries like America which wields a frightful power for good or evil.

Since World War I many books have been written on general education. Most of them have added impetus to a healthy reform. Some of them have made welcome additions to our repertory of techniques. A very few, however, have clarified our vision of a larger strategy, a *mission* that might enable us to marshal our techniques, so as to make an adequate attack on the fundamental problem of modern society. Among those very few books is this little one by the Spanish thinker, José Ortega y Gasset. His may prove in fact to have been the boldest and yet the soundest contribution of our times, striking at the very heart of the problem.

For the heart of the problem appears to be a matter of compatibility among the aims of the myriad individuals who make up the modern world. Their orientation must be such that their collective choices will bring about certain conditions of civilized society, on which the individual, though supremely important, is totally dependent for his opportunity to live a happy or even a peaceful life. As modern world society brings us together in a growing dependence on one another, more and more of the choices we make have a rebounding effect on other individuals and other nations : for example, the choices that will nourish or destroy the seeds of a third world war. What we need is to make possible a general working agreement on choices of this far-reaching sort. Now any agreement imposed by a " master-folk ", or even a group of experts irresponsible to the people, is absolutely useless. It fails to square with the best knowledge we have of ethics, government, anthropology, and human psychology. The agreement must be voluntary, then. But how is voluntary agreement to be reached unless we can agree on the basis for picking the best alternative that is open to us ? In real life the trouble usually is not any disagreement on such ultimate objectives as freedom from disease, the self-fulfilment of the individual, or liberty and justice for all. The disagreement is rather over the question as to which alternative will best lead to these objectives, which one will *work* the best. Voluntary agreement therefore must rest on a common understanding of the physical and social conditions under which we are striving to carry out our objectives. If someone objects that the trouble is selfishness rather than ignorance, the answer is that narrow, socially harmful purposes are merely secondary effects of ignorance. For in our time at least, these narrow purposes are not defensible even on grounds of self-interest.

We find around us, obviously, too little common understanding and no ready means by which diverse cultures, or even diversely trained individuals in our own culture, can bring themselves to a common plateau of knowledge from which they might reason their way on together to a working agreement upon a next step. Modern knowledge does not make this common understanding an easy matter. In fact, it almost defies the capacity of the human intellect, not only because it is constantly expanding at such a dizzy rate, but still more because in the past, at a number of successive stages, it has emitted conflicting interpretations, and these survive in the present world to add to our confusion. The commonest human reaction to this difficult heritage has been, as we might expect, to evade the challenge and not attempt any comprehensive grasp of it. Most of us have dodged the greater part of our many-sided responsibility for being enlightened citizens of the modern global community. In the momentous choices of the last two decades, we have " rebelled " against the burden of knowing what would be the wisest next step, according to the best knowledge of our times.

We have acted not as responsible individuals but as a part of " the masses ".

Ortega's restless genius was already analysing this very problem in *La Rebelión de las Masas*, published in 1929, and was pushing on to seek a solution of the problem in the present study, which was completed and published in 1930. This was before the Depression had led the rest of us to look for the deeper significance of World War I in the underlying cultural disequilibrium of our whole civilization. It is only now in fact that our general-education movement, spurred on by a third upheaval, is penetrating to the deeper questions of the problem. How can the present partial insights be synthesized to form the basis of some common understanding, evolving yet stable ? How can a synthesis be taught without undermining the very freedom it is intended to serve ?

The general-education movement in the United States stands out for its advances in pedagogical techniques, guidance, survey courses, integration of courses, and even general curricula, which however belie one another's claim to any comprehensive integration. We have been developing these techniques in a spirit of unrealistic optimism despite all our protestations to the contrary. It took a blow that shattered our faith in automatic progress to make us buckle down to the basic questions that worried Ortega a decade and a half ago. Thus for a second time the hardy, practical-minded pioneers of our country, as they push back one of the great frontiers of history, find stretching on before them the trail of an imaginative Spanish explorer.

This suggestion of the book's importance and timeliness would be sufficient introduction were it not that the sketchy little volume takes on much of its meaning from a very complex background in the life and thought of its author. To project the sketch against an imagined background would fill it in with wrong colours—all the more so, if one has sensed that the colouring ought to be good and bold.

The life of Ortega is complicated by no less than five parallel careers. He is at once a teacher, an essayist, a publisher-editor, a philosopher, and a statesman. And his life has been further complicated by the turbulent surrounding history and a web of causal interconnections. Clearly, therefore, the best judgments we can make at present must be put forth very modestly—a caution which not all writers on the subject have observed.

Furthermore the present introduction will have to skip here and there in the large subject, in order to pick out the points that shed the most light on Ortega's theory of cultural education.

For the life of Ortega from 1883, the year of his birth, to the outbreak of the Spanish Civil War in 1936, we may fortunately refer to an excellent biographical sketch by Mrs. Helene Weyl, one of his translators who knows him well. This is available in the *University of Toronto Quarterly* of July, 1937 (pages 461–479). For the years from 1936 on, the world will probably have to wait a number of years for a definitive biography. It would be easy enough to enlarge upon the salient events of his life during this period, which Professor Federico de Onís, the eminent Columbia bibliographer and a friend of Ortega's from boyhood, has graciously summarized for us in a letter of August, 1943. Ortega was deathly ill when he left Spain, shortly after the outbreak of the Civil War, and made his way to Paris where he underwent a serious operation. He moved on next to Holland to recuperate, thence to Portugal, and to Argentina for a longer stay. In 1942 he decided to return to Portugal.

What matters most, however, is not the narrative of his life but its interpretation, and this grows the more precarious after 1936 for a new reason : Ortega himself has been comparatively silent during this period of protracted illness. Hence the editorial reactions of the press, which have sometimes been stormy, are more difficult than ever to evaluate. They not only may be biased ; they may even rest upon an inexact knowledge of what Ortega had said in the first place. This is particularly true of the documents relating to Ortega's last visit to the western hemisphere. The inner explanation of all tempests must await the reflective analysis of some very level-headed historian.

These last eight years, however, are comparatively unimportant as background for *Mission of the University*. The period that concerns us here is the quarter of a century stretching from about 1910 up to 1936. During those years Ortega enjoyed full opportunity to express his torrential flow of ideas, and so he has left us a very complete record. But here again the critics seem unable to agree on any elements of an evaluation. Why is it that judgments of Ortega range from such ardent devotion to almost equally ardent deprecation, with such a comparatively sparse distribution of opinions over the middle ground ? It is true that we are all more narrowly specialized than Ortega and so we naturally incline to focus our attention on one side or another of his vast activity. But that does not explain why each of his activities is so variously judged. The essential explanation seems to be less a matter of reason than one of emotion. The fact is that it is impossible for Ortega's contemporaries to view him dispassionately. His fiery personality, and his persistent relevance to the burning questions in our own lives, make him a controversial subject. Even within himself, his several careers and the characteristics they have developed in him react on one another, and generate an imbroglio of epic proportions. The spectator loses all spirit of detachment as he takes sides in this one-man drama of the modern mind.

Ortega's volubility and varied public contacts as a journalist might have passed as natural to the type, if only the teacher in him were not so prone to correct the misconceptions he encountered. The same pedagogical trait, reacting with his developed social consciousness, gave rise to an unusual amount of friction even in his teaching career. For he was so keenly aware of the practical consequences of ideas that he could never be satisfied to teach social ethics as merely pretty theories. Again, Ortega was undeniably skilful as a political figure, yet in that career his propensity for instructing people made him quite unable either to compromise suavely with his opponents or to let himself be led expediently by his followers.

Even these careers might not have clashed as they did, were it not for the philosopher's loyalty to a many-sided truth that satisfies no partisan mind. Ortega is to be classed as a conservative in politics, but one who has his own independent ideas on what is most worth conserving in our complex heritage. As a result he has been severely critical of the left and the right alike, and both sides have taken his criticism for evidence that he had joined the opposing camp. In the Civil War he objected bitterly to the use of Spain by both fascists and communists as the unlucky testing ground for the implements of the next world war. He condemned the leaders at home, the leaders abroad, and even the foreigners themselves, for as he saw it they were intruding in Spain with their public opinion, grossly ignorant of what Spain and the Spanish people really needed. Communism and fascism alike, transplanted into the Spanish mind, simply clouded the issue and delayed the solution. Subsequent history appears to reveal considerable truth in his views, however distasteful they were to both leftists and reactionaries at the time.

From the beginning of his long public life, Ortega exhibits

the same explosive combination of keen analysis and a fearless readiness to show his contemporaries the error of their ways. He antagonized people in power by assailing their abuses of privilege and he disturbed the champions of the underdog by pointing to the incompetence of the " mass man " for true democracy, and deducing that modern society needed the leadership of some aristocracy of the intellect. Obviously an intellectual himself in the best sense, a critical and independent mind, he stood aloof from the practising anti-intellectuals of his time, the totalitarians. Yet he offended his fellow intellectuals constantly by berating " the frivolity and irresponsibility which are frequent in the European ' intellectual ', which I have denounced as a factor of the first magnitude amongst the causes of the present disorder." [1]

That is why it is so difficult for us of to-day to see Ortega dispassionately. If he rises above partisan or professional boundaries, he does so by way of showing up the inadequacies of many types of credo, among which those of most of his critics are necessarily distributed.

And then Ortega's manner of expressing himself makes him difficult to read in an objective spirit. He is skilful in the art of arousing the ordinary reader to think along with the printed page, even when he has a highly sophisticated and complex idea in his own mind. Yet the rhetorical devices he uses for this purpose are sometimes irritating to the seasoned critic—devices like the striking paradoxes which he resolves by an unexpected redefinition of terms ; or such a fiction as the " mass-man ", the economic man's posthumous brother ; or his way of tussling with the meanings of words, or with the supposed stubbornness of the reader, forms of dramatization which are extraneous to the essential line of thought. Good critics have been led to misjudge Ortega, I think, under the influence of negative effects produced by all this technique on their educated taste. Mr. Henry Hazlitt, who was literary editor of the New York *Nation* when *The Modern Theme* was first published in America, in 1933, took that occasion to express his wonderment at the extravagant praise which had greeted *The Revolt of the Masses* a year before, and went so far as to judge Ortega not a real thinker but a ' rhetorician-thinker '. It seems nearer the truth to regard him as a rhetorician *and* a thinker.

The Revolt has been so successful as rhetoric, that in many an American public library it is the most battered volume of all

[1] " Concerning Pacifism," *Nineteenth Century*, 124 (July, 1938), p. 32.

hose which have attempted, in the past decade, to convince the ordinary citizen of his cultural incompetence. It has done its part towards obtaining the public support on which the general-education movement depends. Ortega the journalist has been a shrewd judge of that wide public which demands dramatized ideas, and induces the writer to press home main points rather than to draw fine distinctions and weigh each cautious allegation.

On the other hand, *The Revolt* has not appealed to the un-critical reader alone. Among the American educators who have referred to it with appreciation in their own writings are George Edgar Vincent, Norman Foerster, Robert Shafer, and Henry M. Wriston. Its essential line of thought has been generally re-affirmed, not only by thinkers, but by subsequent history. Cer-tainly the decade of the thirties has been one unhappy chronicle of the retreat of humane values and enlightened ideas, weakly defended, and brutally misunderstood and derided by geniuses educated to gross ideals.

Ortega the thinker is not to be dismissed, therefore, either because Ortega the journalist writes in a showmanlike style or because Ortega the political figure invokes our partisan feelings. If his tempestuous combination of careers makes him difficult to evaluate coolly, perhaps his very breadth of experience may have led him to some larger insights that a narrower view of life would never have inspired. In the field of education there is particular reason to look to such a background as Ortega's for some fruitful ideas. To-day few thinkers can venture into the wider reaches of school and society without becoming dangerously unskilled amateurs. And so it is not amiss for us to approach with expecta-tion and humility this extraordinary thinker, whose personal experience spreads to the four corners of the vast subject.

Few other modern philosophers, and possibly none, have achieved such popular leadership as Ortega exerted during the Spanish Republic of the nineteen-thirties. He came, in fact, to be called by many of his fellow citizens " the father of the Re-public ". On the fall of the dictator Primo de Rivera in 1931, Ortega organized a number of Spanish intellectuals into a " League for the Service of the Republic ". This took him into politics, for as the delegate of this League he was elected to the Constituent Cortes. Thus he gained a valuable knowledge of public affairs, the possibilities and limitations of the governing process, and the nature of political leadership.

This knowledge he added to an already rich experience of active life as a publisher and journalist. For he had founded and edited the world-famous magazine, *Revista de Occidente* ; and he had helped to found the newspaper *El Sol* and the publishing house Espasa-Calpe, both of which likewise earned a world-wide reputation. As an essayist, he has appealed to a very wide public with scores of delightful adventures of ideas. They begin often with some everyday experience common to all of us, and carry the reader to some pregnant idea about life—twentieth-century Spectator Papers, which in fact are collected into a series of volumes called *El Espectador*. He has succeeded too in getting the general public to consider his more ambitious theses. The wide appeal of his *Revolt of the Masses* and *Modern Theme* we can observe in the United States.

So Ortega is well aware of that general public which condemns to death educational institutions that forget their dependence on the society outside. And this fact intercepts any hasty judgment one might be led to make of the present essay. Despite the caveat Ortega introduces on pages 37–8, 40 and 76–8, several readers of the manuscript have still remained unconvinced. They express the opinion that Ortega seems, at points, to regard culture as a river that takes its rise in the lofty university and flows down over the plains and swamp-lands below. Yet it is safe to assume that he is thoroughly conscious of society, and that in building the skeletal structure he presents here, he has had in mind how it would lend itself to a fruitful interplay between the university's organized critical knowledge and the lessons men learn in the school of experience.

Ortega's fiction of presenting this essay as a mere collection of notes written for his own use has this much truth in it : the essay makes no pretence of meeting the obvious queries which other minds will be sure to raise. It calls for a twofold activity of our imagination. First of all, what made him jot down these particular headings and broken sentences, on the scraps of paper we can imagine, and why did he arrange them in this sequence ? And secondly, as to the ramifications he has omitted to mention, did he think they were so obvious that he was sure to remember them, or did he really forget to take them into account ? Perhaps our difficulties on these points find their compensation in the brevity of the essay, and in the intimate glimpses we catch here and there of a great mind at work.

As a teacher Ortega has had a long and eminently successful career. After years of unhurried preparation, largely in Spain and in Germany, he was appointed in 1911 to the Chair of Metaphysics at the University of Madrid. This post he occupied for some twenty-five years, with one short interruption when he resigned in protest against the dictatorship's encroachment on academic freedom. He has been an inspiring teacher, whose students were willing to follow him outside the university when he found the atmosphere of its halls too turbulent for scholarship.

Ortega's success in teaching has been due in considerable part to two dominant characteristics.

The one is his ingenious way of starting from everyday experience, just as he does in the *Spectator* essays, to arrive at some general idea which henceforth takes on a new significance. Like Alfred North Whitehead, Ortega knows the art of " suffusing knowledge with imagination " by bringing the abstract into contact with the particular. Like Whitehead again, he is accustomed to " seek simplicity but distrust it ". When he proposes that young people should learn a body of previously formulated concepts, therefore, we would be wrong to imagine that he has in mind a process of learning by rote a system of verbalizations presumed to represent truths. The place of a synthesis in teaching would be simply to make the inevitable influence of the teacher more responsible to the best knowledge our age can provide, and more effective in speeding the student's discovery of the problems and his arrival at responsible views of his own.

Ortega's other great characteristic as a teacher confirms the belief that this is how he would go about building a synthesis into a student's cultural education. He is above all a teacher of individuals. It has been interesting to question several former students of his whom I have met during the past seven years. They all mention that he liked best to work with pupils in small groups. He let them do their investigating for themselves but he was an exacting critic of what they brought back. Without requiring any individual to believe as he did, he inspired his pupils to surpass themselves in power, knowledge, and humane purposiveness. As they look back on his teaching, they feel that they developed their own individuality rather than lost any of it, and if he induced them to broaden their personality in the process, he was simply calling into play some of their latent potentialities. Ortega's practice leaves no doubt that he takes for granted the

guided self-development of individuals as the very life process o
any good educational institution.

As a teacher, therefore, Ortega has been quite the opposit
of the mass-minded educator one might infer him to be from
reading *Mission of the University* by itself.[1] His theory is no
a description of his practice, but rather a supplement to it. Ir
Ortega's case this was inevitable, because he was not in a positioi
to carry out more than a part of his theory. He appreciated
fully that education must be individualized, that it must be made
available to the whole electorate of modern society, and that it;
content must be made responsible to the best knowledge of al
fields of learning. The first part of the programme, the in-
dividualization, he was able to carry out by himself. For the
other two parts, however, the universalization of opportunity
and the synthesis, he needed the co-operation of many voters,
officials, and trained specialists in many fields of learning ; and
in his generation neither the public, the officials, nor the specialist;
were ready to play their part.

Do his practices in real life contradict his theory of a cultural
synthesis ? The answer appears to be no. Certainly individualized education is not a substitute for formulating a
rational standard of social awareness. Neither is universalization
of the opportunity to learn. All three are necessary.

The other element of Ortega's practice, his method of beginning from particulars, seems harder to square with his proposal
for a synthesis of preformulated ideas. Yet the truth is that the
need for synthesis has arisen precisely from this kind of thinking.
Suppose you resolve with Ortega to generalize only from established, particular experiences, and to think your way through
from these to generalizations comprehensive enough to serve as
guides for your life. You open up immediately the vexed
questions of the modern mind. What constitutes a valid point
of departure, an irreducible perception ? What assumptions are
involved in our reasoning and how do they vary from one culture
to another ? What limitations are inherent in our human
reasoning, conceived as one of the processes of an organism's

---

[1] In the earlier *Biología y Pedagogía* (San José de Costa Rica : J. García Monge,
1923. 77 pp.), on the contrary, Ortega appears as an educator concerned primarily
with the individual. For that book was written in order to oppose a law requiring
Don Quixote to be read in primary schools ; and the ground for Ortega's opposition
was that such a requirement was incompatible with education conceived as the
growth of the individual child. (Sr. Domingo Casanovas offers an excellent brief
summary of *Biología y Pedagogía* in *Educación* [Caracas, Venezuela], May-June 1940,
pp. 26–8.)

adaptation to its environment ? What limitations does the world
outside impose on our formulations of truth, in addition to those
inherent in our own nature ? What are the generalizations
called " values ", according to which we order our lives, and to
what extent can values and the means of establishing values be
agreed upon ? And what should we do, rationally speaking, in
those areas of our life where no rational conclusions are to be
had ?

On these basic questions a mere personal opinion is not
enough, if diverse individuals and cultures are to have any common understanding of what is worth co-operating for, what is
possible in the light of our physical and biological knowledge,
and what alternative means, in the applied and social sciences,
can be reasonably selected and put into effect. A narrower
specialist than Ortega may consider one field or another to be
unimportant for his enlightenment. Ortega knows enough to
see that many fields are essential and, furthermore, that before
the restricted scientific conclusions of one field of knowledge can
safely be applied to life, the bearing of the other fields must be
considered within the comprehensive frame of reference called
philosophy or religion.

Thus his theory that a synthesis is necessary not only supple-
ments his practice. It follows from it as an inescapable
consequence.

A modern synthesis of vital knowledge would be an evolving
or " dynamic " synthesis, no more static in form than in content,
and only partially uniform from one mind to the next. It
would include some propositions, but also many open questions.
It could be appealed to only in a critical spirit, and any attempt
to describe it would be adequate only with respect to some
purpose it was designed to serve—just as a description of the
heavens, simplified and organized around some points taken
more or less arbitrarily as centres, might help us to understand
astronomy but could never aspire to portray the whole complex
truth with any completeness or finality.

These limitations of a modern synthesis are familiar enough
to Ortega. As a matter of fact, he is further removed than
most of us from the ancient conception that θεωρία, or theorizing,
results in generalizations that express absolute and universal
facts about reality. Among thinking people of Spanish culture,
Ortega's chief claim to eminence is his insight into the complex

evolution of human civilizations, and his interpretation of the significance of this knowledge for the values of our own times.

Ortega's closest spiritual forebear is Wilhelm Dilthey, a philosopher of the University of Berlin whom Ortega has called " the most important German thinker of the second half of the nineteenth century " [1]—to the conspicuous neglect of Nietzsche, who is much better known in our country as well as in the Nazi Germany he helped to inspire. It is interesting to see that our American historians of ideas are coming to join Ortega in regarding Dilthey as one of the greatest figures in this field of knowledge.

The long eclipse of Dilthey can be accounted for by a conspiracy of three circumstances. He was chronically unable to finish a project, for the same reason as Pascal : his insatiable imagination was forever pushing ahead to new reaches of his problem, and his ideas seemed out of date in his own mind before he could get them into books.

Then, Dilthey was unfortunate in a second generation of interpreters, like Windelband and Rickert and Troeltsch, who lacked the master's acute penetration. They mummified his philosophy. They made it merely one more limited world view while Dilthey had tried, on the contrary, to visualize a sort of comparative anatomy of world views. He had sought to discover how they differ from one another, what they have in common, the secret of their internal organization and their peculiar multi-linear evolution, and finally what basis there may be for comparing their points of excellence, if one rises above the naïve procedure of judging them all by the values inherent in one of them. He saw that it was impossible to consider our own civilization as static or final and that if humanity may be expected to evolve through untold new variations, man may perhaps be able to influence the future of civilization towards undreamed-of realizations of man's higher nature. As we go back to the writings of Dilthey himself instead of the easier interpretations of his thought, we find an unsuspected grandeur and a live concern for problems that remain paramount to-day.

Dilthey's third misfortune was that he was born into a peculiar climate of opinion which somewhat warped the growth of his philosophy of philosophies, in his own mind and in the mind of his great Spanish interpreter. Most philosophers of natural science in the later nineteenth century were following the trend

[1] In " History as a System ", *Towards a Philosophy of History* (W. W. Norton, 1941), p. 216.

of positivism, first to the position of disclaiming any connection between science and values, and then to the still remoter extreme of declining even to have any reference to a real world at all. This simple isolation of the natural sciences appealed to the natural scientists of the period because it seemed to dispense with metaphysics. Rather than avow any metaphysical position they preferred to assume that their science was nothing more than a game of describing and arranging sense perceptions.

This positivistic approach has since lost considerable ground under the attacks of Whitehead and other thinkers of several schools. Some of the positivists themselves, exploring their own position, have rendered it more difficult to maintain. Professor Everett Nelson, for example, appears to have damaged the assumption of his predecessors, that even if we know nothing but sense data we can still make predictions as though we knew we were dealing with a real world. If this assumption is questionable, then the pure positivistic position loses many of its adherents, for obviously we do use our knowledge of the physical world effectively for predictive purposes, and consequently the theory comes into conflict with common sense. To-day the position which regards science as a mere game of arranging sense impressions seems hardly tenable. Yet Dilthey and many of his contemporaries accepted it as the least extravagant assumption available, and Ortega reaffirms the position as late as about 1932 [1] in such terms as these : " To-day we are beginning to see that physics is a mental combination and nothing more " (p. 228). " Physics brings us into contact with no transcendence " (p. 229). " What is real in it—and not mere idea—is only its utility. That is why we have lost our fear of physics, and with our fear our respect, and with respect, our enthusiasm " (p. 229).

This climate of opinion led Dilthey, and Ortega after him, to try to rescue some practical knowledge from the absurd predicament of the sciences. For obviously, if all our knowledge and reasoning should be proved in the same way to be just as remote from reality as physics appeared to be, then we should have to make the adjustment Ortega has made to his view of physics, and abandon our respect and enthusiasm for all knowledge and all rational method. Knowledge would cease to be power, and man would cease trying to be a rational animal. Humanity

[1] The following quotations are from " History as a System ", *Towards a Philosophy of History* (W. W. Norton, 1941).

would yield to a new power and a new animal, just at the threshold of the new world of plenty and well-being that might have been, thanks to a million years or more of piled-up, sifted-down knowledge.

Dilthey felt that this *reductio ad absurdum* was unnecessary by reason of a natural distinction that could be drawn between the sciences and a different kind of knowledge, which he termed *die Geisteswissenschaften*—knowledge relating to the human spirit, or in a word, *the humanities*.[1] He drew a line between the two kinds of knowledge and made the resultant dualism the keystone of his basic philosophy. How much this feature of Dilthey's thought may have had to do with his long eclipse is hard to tell. The present judgment may overestimate its effect. Yet one cannot but sense that even Ortega is hard put to it, in his essay " History as a System ", to distinguish " historical reason " from " scientific reason ". The difficulty of understanding Dilthey's philosophy has been a considerable factor impeding the progress both of Dilthey himself and of his less brilliant followers.

But, apart from Dilthey's literary fortunes, what is the bearing of this background upon a dispassionate appraisal of Ortega's own philosophy? In the first place, Dilthey's thought was of incalculable value since it gave rise to Ortega's key idea of a cultural synthesis. In the second place, its dualism divided and weakened the synthesis. Yet in the last analysis what Dilthey transmitted to his great successor was not a static dualism but an emergent synthesis, already in a state of evolution towards greater inclusiveness.

First, then, Dilthey was absolutely right in drawing the distinction that while the sciences seek to describe relationships within limited frames of reference, the humanities seek to comprehend significances within a frame of reference as large as our whole view of life, including its ideals, its purposes, and its practical decision. To-day it is difficult to express this insight without using the newer vocabulary of Whitehead, yet it is essentially Dilthey's thought. It remains to-day one of our most important ideas on the place of science in the modern mind, and it suggests a level of understanding between scientists and the other fragmentary representatives of the modern mind—in other

---

[1] Dilthey's meaning corresponds primarily to history and criticism, which Professor Joseph Cohen has termed " the interpretive humanities ", as distinguished from " the creative humanities ". The latter field is also to be included, however, for Dilthey emphasized the dependence of interpretation upon a certain empathic experience (*Erlebnis*), which requires a creative act on the part of the critic.

words, a possible synthesis of points of view—far above the level we have attained thus far. Dilthey was profoundly right, moreover, in his endeavour to comprehend the total significance of historic civilizations. If he had not provided a method for this ambitious undertaking, and illustrated the kind of result that can be achieved, Ortega would have lacked the basis he had for proceeding to his second step, the application of Dilthey's method to the problem of understanding our own culture and imparting such understanding to the rising generation.

The sharp dualism of science and the humanities, however, was detrimental to a synthesis of our civilization. We need a rational approach to the conflicting value judgments of the cultures of the world. Even within a single national culture, as it evolves with accelerating rapidity, conflicts are generated that can be resolved only by seeking some mutually convincing, that is, rational basis for co-operation among groups. Dilthey's dualism, on the contrary, has lent itself to the sharp division between ends and means of the fascist philosophers like Pareto : the belief that while we can select our means rationally, ends can only be embraced in a blind and brutish manner that permits no rational selection, no discrimination, and no peaceable reconciliation between ideologies that happen to conflict. The baneful irrationality of fascism consists, in fact, in the employment of powerful rational means towards shamelessly irrational ends—or ends which can be justified only by some peculiar brand of reason, separate from the reason that is employed in science. The foundations of the fascist dualism had been laid long ago, partly by the regrettable, unimaginative hostility of most humanism towards science ever since the Renaissance, and partly by certain elements of our religious traditions. In the late nineteenth century the cleavage was deepened by the reaction of Bergson, Dilthey, Paul Elmer More, and others against the shallow positivism and even shallower scientism of their age.

Meanwhile, the more we have learned of the supposed borderlines between divisions of knowledge, the more impossible it has become to draw any natural line through their interconnected subject matter. In fact the implications of one field for another, even those of technology for human values, seem to be one of our most promising resources. And similarly, the more we study our own mental processes, the more continuous and indivisible we find our essential pattern to be. From the mathematical sciences to biology, from biology to sociology, history, ethics, and the creative arts, we find the same composite process of observation, creative imagination, and a rigorous, logical, critical analysis that constantly rejects the faulty idea or faulty workmanship in favour of a better choice. We must realize, of course, that the twentieth-century conception of an organically unified universe is just as tentative as was the positivistic conception which it appears to supersede. Yet the organismic conception [1] does remove the need for Dilthey's transcendental dualism, and thus clears the way for us to appreciate his really great contribution to our grasp of the place of science in our civilization.

In the last analysis Dilthey did make a great advance in the problem of cultural synthesis. Burckhardt had analysed the culture of the Renaissance before Dilthey, but Burckhardt had run into difficulties as a result of restricting himself too narrowly to the artistic manifestations of the period. Dilthey overcame those difficulties by working out a wider range of causal relationships. Thus the concept of a synthesis which he handed on was an expanding one, and carried within it the momentum to grow still more inclusive. Ortega had the genius to extend the principle from the realm of history to the problem of cultural education in our time. If the cleavage that split Dilthey's synthesis has meanwhile become unnecessary, we are simply more fortunate than Ortega had hoped. If he saw the need and the possibility of a contemporary synthesis despite the rift of content and method which he thought inevitable, is he not all the more extraordinary on that account ?

Besides his intellectual kinship with Dilthey, Ortega bears a close relationship as well with the cyclical historians of his own generation. He is no exception to the striking generalization that all the great philosophers of history in the twentieth century have adopted the theory that history moves by great cycles, made up of successive phases that follow one another in a predictable sequence and with a semblance of rhythm. Like Spengler, Sorokin, and Arnold Toynbee, Ortega sees the pregnant significance of the discovery that history *has* a morphology, and that cultures mature and decline. He shares their pessimistic analysis of the present situation, and their poignant realization of the fact that man is not only or even predominantly a rational

---

[1] A succinct account of this point of view will be found in *The Philosophy of Alfred North Whitehead*, edited by P. A. Schilpp (1941), pp. 256 ff. of the essay contributed by Joseph Needham.

animal, but passional as well. This idea, in fact, furnished the point of departure for Ortega's early book, *The Modern Theme*.[1] In *The Revolt*, Ortega gives a prominent place to the emotional side of human nature. The main constructive idea of the book appears in Chapter XIV, where he looks to some all-consuming social purpose as the only force that could bring together the individuals of to-day in a thriving social order.

Even in *The Revolt*, however, Ortega is not defeatist or fatalistic. The prospect of a highly purposive society governed by the people is a friendly one, even if the people are led by their emotions, in comparison with the " new Caesarism " of Spengler, the sensual barbarism into which we are plunging according to Sorokin, or the wave of religiosity that Toynbee seems to antici-pate, if we may judge by the volumes that have appeared of his great *Study of History*. In *Mission of the University*, Ortega departs further from the sinister outlook of his compeers and rejects most of the anti-rational implications of the cyclical theory. Not that he loses sight of the passional element which had featured so largely in the descriptive studies of *The Revolt*, a year before. He simply shifts his attention to the constructive problem of how modern democratic society can select and favour the best emotional reactions, the best purposes, the best decisions our times make possible. His hypothesis is that this depends on the use we make of our reason. That is why his analysis of the stormy con-temporary world brings him with his problem into the quiet precinct of the university : not because he is at home only in this sector of society but because the university is the embodiment of the Western man's determination to live according to his intellect. On the university falls the responsibility of leadership in the two processes requisite for an effective reform of general education : first to synthesize the best of our culture, and second, to make this basis for enlightened living an influence for good throughout all the specialized forms of modern life.

Ortega admits that we have no assurance of success ; this admission is a part of his " sober spirit of reform ". And here he meets with general agreement, for the most fatalistic among us seem to admit that it is nobler to strive than not, even in the face of heavy odds against us. But in order to make his con-structive proposal, Ortega ventures far beyond this rudimentary

[1] Early among Ortega's books, though he was 40 in that year, 1923. It is significant that this book appeared just as the dictatorship came into power, while *The Revolt* and its constructive counterpart appeared successively in the last two years before the fall of the dictatorship and the establishment of the republic.

point of agreement. His outlook may be congenial to our idea
of the world we would like to bequeath to our children, but is it
to be trusted, and are we to trust our own biased judgment of
what it is wise and practicable to work for ?

There seem to be several reasons for Ortega's deviation from
the prophetic inferences of the other cyclical historians ; and the
reasons point to a possibility that he might have the larger insight
after all.

In the first place his peculiarly wide experience gives him an
advantage in the imponderable but highly important matter of
general emotional disposition. Among the inbred professional
points of view in modern society, the historians occupy a position
of extreme pessimism, challenged perhaps only by the bankers.
The other end of the scale must be accorded to the social planners
and reformers, their closest second being, doubtless, the engineers.
This fanciful arrangement need not be passed off as a scientific
study of group attitudes. There is enough truth in it as it is to
make one stop and think whether Ortega, whose background
embraces both of the extreme traditions, may not have a more
balanced perspective than the specialist whose opinions are
strongly coloured by reading and contacts in the one tradition
or the other.

Ortega's active life also afforded him a wide first-hand experience of people, and thus overcame a kind of ignorance that
appears to be the mainstay of most academic pessimism. Contact with the people, through his essay writing and his politics,
taught him what many a professor is learning to-day through
participation in the community forums and committees of our
expanding adult education : namely, that the public at large
is not nearly so unthinking, unimaginative, short-sighted, irresponsible, or esthetically ignoble as he had pictured it in his cloistered
imaginings.

In the second place, Dilthey's influence accounts for an
important difference in approach between Ortega and the other
cyclical historians. Spengler and Toynbee, together with most
of the lesser lights, have concerned themselves primarily with the
analogies that may be discovered between the historic civilizations. Their effort has been to graph the rise and fall of cultures
and to establish by induction a composite, schematized curve.
In their forecast of the future they have been guided above all
by the course of this theoretical curve. They place upon it the
curve of our own civilization, plot the point where they think we

stand at the present moment, and proceed to extrapolate the remainder of a melancholy decline. Ortega, on the other hand, has been concerned above all to comprehend sympathetically the meaning of our own present civilization, by dint of patient contemplation and analysis. One of his numerous studies illustrating this attitude is " The Dehumanization of Art ", translated in M. M. Rader, *A Modern Book of Esthetics* (Henry Holt and Company, 1935).

Hence Ortega is more impressed with what is peculiar to our age—in the light of its evolutionary background, of course —while Spengler and Toynbee are inclined to attribute less importance than he to those unique factors which might conceivably cause our civilization to deviate far from the generic curve. Perhaps Ortega is neglecting one of the clearest lessons of history. But on the other hand, is it not rash to trust implicitly to the extrapolation of a theoretical curve, which even in engineering is a most precarious means of forecasting ?

It is possible that Ortega is less out of line than he may seem. Spengler's famous view of civilizations as being discontinuous from one another and mutually incomprehensible is not the only interpretation of the evidence. Toynbee's more elaborate study has led rather to the opinion that there has been considerable continuity from one civilization to the next, and that a creative minority in our present time can exact an appreciable influence on the era ahead, even if it is the beginning of a new civilization. Ortega takes this same position in the first chapter of the present book, when he tells his youthful audience of the power they might have as " a group in form ", to lead a reorganization of society in Spain. (One can see here, in passing, how fascism in its early stages might have appealed to an honest liberal preoccupied with the dire need of social reform.)

If Dilthey has perhaps saved Ortega from putting too much trust in the newly discovered curve, he has certainly warned him effectively against taking æsthetics too exclusively as vantage point from which to interpret our whole civilization— though it is true that his own breadth of interests would hardly have let him fall into the fault of Burckhardt. This is precisely the fault, however, which seems to impair Sorokin's interpretation of the present and his forecast of the future. And the same criticism applies to those who would regard Proust as the final summary of all the Western world has achieved, neglecting the important fact that Proust's exquisite partial synthesis leaves quite out of account the vigorous social movements of his time which now seem the elements most likely to generate future history.

In comparison with the dominant emphasis of Sorokin, therefore, as well as that of Spengler and Toynbee, Ortega may have been well advised in adopting Dilthey's preoccupation with *Erlebnis* or empathy.

The most original feature of Ortega's constructive proposal, the idea of a cultural synthesis, appears to be one more result of his endeavour to penetrate into the significance of our present civilization rather than to predict fatalistically the curve of its decline. As he contemplated the happiness and unhappiness he saw around him, he developed convictions that certain elements of our civilization were good and others bad. This development in itself would not have distinguished him from Spengler or Sorokin, whose value judgments are evidenced by a host of such terms as " *decline* of the west " and " *sensate* civilization ". Even those of us who lament that there are no values, in fact, betray indirectly our assumption that another state of affairs would be better—better according to what, if it is not a scale of values? But Ortega deliberately erects his value judgments into a positive concept of life " at the height of the times ", and he confidently marks as bad the elements of the contemporary world that militate against this positive ideal. Hence the title *La Rebelión de las Masas*, by which he means a rebellion, more akin to passive evasion than to revolt, on the part of the ordinary man against the burden of taking a responsible part in modern society according to the best knowledge our age affords.

Ortega would no doubt be quick to admit that his ideas of excellence are " dated ", for few thinkers have been more impressed than he with the constant change in climates of opinion. On the other hand, he could point out that beneath the dated particularizations necessary to his idea of a good society one will find the two interdependent values that have proved the most constant in the whole Judeo-Christian tradition : individual self-realization and social justice. If the point is well taken that we cannot help committing ourselves to value judgments whether we want to or not, then Ortega's course of selecting and refining a positive ideal is no more naïve than a negativistic attitude or a cult of objectivity without admitting that objectivity is thereby being chosen as a value.

Ortega's idea of the good university is far more " dated "

than his idea of a good society. The latter necessarily takes its cue from the persistent needs and wants of mankind, while the institution is proposed as a remedy for a specific defect in contemporary society. Ortega is not to be bracketed with those who urge a return to the university of the thirteenth century on the assumption that this would somehow restore the cultural unity we associate with that age. He is too thorough a scholar to overlook the fact that in the heyday of the medieval universities the teaching of the classics was at a low ebb, and less than half the universities had a faculty of theology to teach first principles, while they all had their law school and most of them a school of medicine. He is also too modest a scholar, for all his positive and imperious manner of arguing, to claim discovery of the model university for all ages.

Ortega's constructive proposal does force him to make one questionable assumption, however, which the fatalists manage to avoid : the assumption that men are rational enough to reject a less tenable idea, in the long run, for a more tenable one.[1] For unless this assumption is true, the university would only waste its pains in attempting to persuade the public of any enlightened idea.

This assumption is certainly the weak point in Ortega's argument. He has himself disparaged the power of rationality as eloquently as anyone, notably in Chapter VIII of *The Revolt* where he berates the rebellious " mass-man " for being so impervious to right reason.[2] But on the other hand, all education above the animal-training level rests on the same assumption. So does democracy. So does justice itself. We can avoid assuming the rationality of a majority, of course, by entrusting all the decisions of society to a few. Arithmetically this results in a more frugal assumption. But in real life it brings with it all the corruption that oligarchies are heir to. Ortega's assumption may be the least of the evils, therefore, unless we prefer to rebel against the whole attempt to live on a human level, and resign ourselves to a life of irrational animality, with the one distinction that our

[1] Ortega expresses this assumption in " History as a System " (*Towards a Philosophy of History*, Norton, 1941), pages 211 and 215. He is no doubt assuming too that men can be educated to follow the pattern of rational choice more consistently and more promptly than they have done in the past. This is certainly a good possibility. Cf. John Dewey's position in *Experience and Education* (1938) pp. 100-1 : " There is nothing in the inherent nature of habit that prevents intelligent method from becoming itself habitual. . . ."

[2] Ortega's analysis here agrees strikingly with E. L. Thorndike's in " The Psychology of the Half-Educated Man ", *Harper's*, 140 (April 1920), pp. 666-70.

animal cunning now enjoys a great mechanical extension of our sheer brute force and five senses.

The crucial test of human rationality will probably come when a synthesis " at the height of the times " is presented to those contemporary cultures which have not, until then, taken much part in its formulation. Here again Ortega and Spengler part company in their analysis and their predictions. Spengler believes that even contemporary cultures like those of Russia and Western Europe are mutually incomprehensible, to such a point that any effort at an understanding on values can lead only to deeper and deeper misunderstandings. Ortega believes on the contrary that when one penetrates beneath the surface manifestations of the contemporary national cultures, one discovers these colourful differences to be merely alternative means for realizing the same universal human aspirations and for solving the same human problems. On this belief he builds a theory that intercultural education can lead to harmony, first by making the most of the common humanity underlying all cultures, and secondly —if we may apply his synthesis idea on this large scale—by disseminating the best knowledge and leading judgments of each field of learning so that, as the diverse cultures evolve, they may come gradually to converge not only on underlying objectives but also in their conditioning ideas of the physical cosmos, of life in the biological sense, and all the instrumental values that can be enlightened by the social and the natural sciences.

What chance there may be for a convergent evolution of cultures on this world-wide scale remains to be found out. It does seem, unfortunately, that where the contemporary cultures differ from one another is not a matter of superior and inferior systems of logic, among which natural selection might be expected to apply. It is rather a matter of conflicting assumptions, or postulates, according to which they conduct their reasoning. By their very nature, one's basic postulates cannot be established rationally ; that would engage the reasoner in an infinite regress. Perhaps the conflict of postulates holds in store an eventual deadlock of misunderstanding such as Spengler has envisaged. On the other hand there is a chance that when alternative postulates confront one another, a rational choice on some pragmatic grounds or other may result ; and this outcome can be strongly favoured by education that points out the advantage to humanity of a reasonable and co-operative spirit.

For the present, we can only conclude that what little we

know of these remote effects of a cultural synthesis is not enough to count very much, either for or against our starting out on the road Ortega opens up. We can however see clearly three great immediate problems which all require a synthesis for their solution.

One is the problem of science itself, which runs the danger of declining into a wasteful repetition of results already attained, unless our present knowledge can be more effectively organized.[1] For this purpose a merely descriptive synthesis might be enough, were it not for the interdependence of the fields of knowledge for so many of their generalizations, and the overwhelming number of data that are consequently involved. In view of this, the sciences themselves need not a merely descriptive but a dynamic synthesis which interprets the data according to concepts of causality and relative significance. Moreover, in so far as the scientist selects data or conclusions for their significance to human life, he is rising to the still higher and more precarious level of a cultural synthesis ; for that term means, essentially, the selection and organization of knowledge relating to the conduct of human life.

The second problem whose solution depends on a cultural synthesis is that of social planning. Liberals and conservatives alike admit that we are engaged in this dangerous use of reason, and that the project is an expanding one. They agree too that we have less chance of controlling our monster of technology by any other means. But, to any extent that we propose to direct the course of human events, we entrust ourselves to the accuracy and completeness of our own knowledge. We must formulate an effective working knowledge of the many fields involved in social planning, therefore, on pain of causing great human misery through our very effort to relieve it.

The third problem requiring a cultural synthesis is the underlying one of general education with which we opened this introductory discussion. The reasons for believing that a synthesis is necessary in this area have been indicated already, and Ortega will develop them further in his essay.

To those who doubt the feasibility of any cultural synthesis, the only answer is that the question will have to be decided by experiment. For the past three years, such an experiment has

[1] Professor Melville H. Hatch has indicated how acute this problem is in his own field of biology, citing the fact that in 1940 the Library of the Marine Biological Station at Woods Hole, Massachusetts, was receiving no less than 1,257 periodicals of interest to biologists.

been under way in a " synthesis seminar " at the University of Washington, a group which includes faculty representatives recruited from some twenty departments or colleges of the University, three church leaders, and some able graduates and upper classmen enrolled in the seminar, " analysis of the modern cultural crisis ".   So far the evidence points towards the possibility of a very valuable synthesis of values, principles of method, and concepts relating to the nature of the world, man, and civilization.   The group has explored contradictory notions of human nature arising, for example, from the partial insights of economics, history, and anthropology.   To bring these together and define their respective fields of validity is certainly of value to education, social planning, and research.   The discussion of science and religion has revealed that the animosity between the naturalists and the liberal religionists was due not to the beliefs of either, but rather to beliefs that each was attributing to the other out of sheer ignorance.   The constructive possibilities of this discovery for contemporary community life need not be dwelt upon.

It is likely that war conditions will lead many college faculties to work systematically on the problem of general education. Already there is competition among our institutions of higher learning to claim that they have some standard of proficiency in general education as in the professional fields, instead of the usual pathetic standard of mere alternative fragments.   None of the more ready-made devices we have tried is either so logical a remedy for the real trouble, or so inviting an adventure of research and comradeship, as the avenue of approach that we owe to the genius of Ortega.

HOWARD LEE NOSTRAND.

MISSION OF THE UNIVERSITY

TO THE F. U. E. OF MADRID

The Federación Universitaria Escolar of Madrid asked me to give a lecture on some topic related to the reform of higher education. The very poor acoustics of the Paraninfo, however, and my poor health at the time, prevented me from developing adequately the theme of my lecture. This circumstance prompted me afterwards to rewrite somewhat more amply the notes I had taken with me to the Paraninfo. And here you have the result. It will be seen that except for an introduction, which the student mind of that time made necessary, I have kept rigorously to what I consider the crucial question. I was anxious to advance this question for discussion, and the pages which follow make no pretence of being anything more than the material for an extensive debate. Accordingly, I have set down my ideas with exaggerated sharpness and simplicity.

In no respect do I flatter myself that I have treated the theme of higher education with any sort of adequacy. The present essay is to be considered only as an anticipation of some future course on the Idea of the University. A definitive study calls first of all for a clear description of the essential characteristics of our age and an accurate diagnosis of the rising generation.

CHAPTER I

A TEMPERED SPIRIT OF REFORM

The Federation of University Students asked me to come here and speak to you on the reform of education.[1] Now I loathe speaking in public, to such an extent that I have managed to do so very few times in my life. Yet this time, without a moment's hesitation, I let myself be corralled by the students. Which shows with what enthusiasm I have come here. In fact, I come with great enthusiasm, but with small faith. For it is clear that these are two different things. Man would be badly off, indeed, if he were incapable of enthusiasm except for the things in which he has faith! Humanity would still be pursuing its existence in a hole in the ground ; for everything that has made it possible to emerge from the cave and the primeval jungle appeared in its first hour as a highly dubious undertaking. Nevertheless, man has been able to grow enthusiastic over his vision of these unconvincing enterprises. He has put himself to work for the sake of an idea, seeking by magnificent exertions to arrive at the incredible. And in the end, he has arrived there. Beyond all doubt it is one of the vital sources of man's power, to be thus able to kindle enthusiasm from the mere glimmer of something improbable, difficult, remote. The other sort of enthusiasm, cradled comfortably by faith, is hardly worthy of the name, because it is sure of its success from the outset. Little is to be expected from the man who exerts himself only when he has the certainty of being recompensed in the end! I remember having written in 1916 that the Germans would lose the war, because they had entered it too sure of victory : their mind was wholly on the conquering, and not simply on fighting. One must go into any kind of struggle prepared for anything, including calamity and defeat. For these, as much as victory, are masks life can put on in a moment. Every day the conviction forces itself on me with new clarity, that too much security demoralizes men more than anything else. Because they came to feel too secure, all the aristocracies of history have fallen into

[1] EDITOR'S NOTE : Mrs. Helene Weyl dates this address " late in the autumn, or more likely, in the early winter of 1930 ". The present book, which was published soon after the lecture, bears the date 1930, and speaks of the *Rebelión de las Masas* as " recientemente publicado ". The first edition of the *Rebelión*, though dated 1929, has a colophon stating that the printing was finished August 26, 1930.

irreparable degeneracy. And one of the ailments of the present time, particularly of the rising generation, is that the modern man, thanks to technological progress and social organization, is inclined to feel sure of too many things about his life.[1]

Do not be surprised therefore that I come before you, according to an old peculiarity of human nature, with more enthusiasm than faith. But why do I have so little faith? Let me tell you. It is now close to twenty-five years since I wrote my first articles on the reform of the Spanish state in general and the university in particular—articles which won me the friendship of Don Francisco Giner de los Ríos. In those days, you could count on your fingers all the people in Spain who admitted the necessity of reforming either the state or the university. Anyone who dared speak of reform, or even insinuate that it was appropriate, was *ipso facto* declared a madman and an outlaw. He was cast off on a tangent from the circle of normal Spanish society, regardless of who he might be, and condemned to a marginal existence, as if reform were leprosy. Do not think that this hostility towards the slightest suspicion of reform arose because the reformers were a radical lot, a menace to society, etc., etc. Not at all. The most moderate of men would have been ostracized for the mention of reform. Such was the case of Antonio Maura, who had been raised to the height of power by the conservatives themselves. Convinced that even the most conservative point of view required changes in the organization of the state, Maura found himself suddenly relegated to the periphery of the national life. His attempt at reform was crushed by a witticism in vogue at the time, comparing him to a rural policeman in a china shop. Two things escaped the wits who bandied this joke about—one, that in a few years their china shop was to be invaded by the whole police force on horseback ; and the other, that they revealed a stubborn determination on their own part to preserve a *status quo* which had about it, indeed, all the frailty of chinaware.

I cite this notorious example to indicate the general, hidebound obstinacy which opposed the reform of anything then in power in Spain, including the state and the university. Those of us who advocated change and proposed to revise antiquated forms were called again and again " enemies of the University." For supporting new institutions like the *Residencia de Estudiantes*, which was created precisely to promote the welfare of the

[1] AUTHOR'S NOTE : On this matter see my recent book *The Revolt of the Masses*.

university by stimulating the ferment of thought, we were dubbed the university's official enemies. To-day, of course, those who reviled the loudest are just the people who hasten to imitate the *Residencia de Estudiantes*. In this they deserve nothing but praise. But at the same time it is only fair to recall that, for many years, gibes and insults were the portion of those who felt some honest concern for the Spanish university and were determined that it should not continue indefinitely to be the sad, inert, spiritless thing it then was. For candour obliges one to observe that our university to-day is decidedly different from what it was, though it is still far from what it ought to be, and can be.

At present, throughout all our national life, the constellations have changed. Hard-fisted facts have come to silence the carping mouths and convince the slowest among us that government and university alike need reform : it is not a question of desiring reform or not ; it is imperative that we make an effort, because neither of these institutions is working. They are machines worn out by the wear and tear of use and abuse.

To-day we are not alone. Many people desire the transformation of the Spanish body politic, and those who do not are resigned to bear with it, somehow or other. Certainly the moment is full of opportunity. You do not appreciate, young people, what good fortune you have had : you have come into life at a magnificent juncture in the destinies of Spain—when the horizon lies open, and many, many great things are going to be possible, among them a new state and a new university. It would be difficult to be more optimistic than I am concerning the interpretation to be put on the current situation of the country. Events which nearly everyone has viewed with alarm seem to me to be ironical masks, under whose evil appearance are hidden really favourable developments. Certainly the moment is full of opportunity ; you have come at the dawn of an illustrious era. A people dormant for centuries is beginning to stir, with those sleepy, jerking motions of a person about to awake and rise to his feet. The moment can be happily described by that very expressive line of poetry, in which the venerable poem of the Cid relates the dawning of a day :

Apriessa cantan los gallos e quieren crebrar albores . . .[1]

Then has not the moment arrived for joining a new faith

---

[1] " Abruptly, cocks begin to crow, the light of dawn is about to break " (*Poema de mio Cid*, line 235).

with the old enthusiasm ?   To this I must answer, provisionally, " No, . . . not yet." In my optimism, it strikes me as clear and definite that the horizon which lies open before the Spaniard of to-day is a magnificent one.   Now the horizon is a symbol of possibilities, presenting themselves before our human life. And this life of ours, in its turn, is a process of converting these possibilities into actual realities.   Here is the point where my optimism falters, and my faith fails me.   For in history—in life —possibilities do not become realities of their own accord ; someone, with his hands and his brain, with his labour and his self-sacrifice, must make realities of them.   History and life, for this reason, are a perpetual *creating*.   Our life is not given to us ready-made : in a fundamental sense it is, precisely, what we are constantly and continuously making of ourselves.   The process is going on at every instant.   Nothing is ours outright, as a gift ; we have to perform for ourselves even those of our actions which seem most passive.   The humble Sancho Panza kept suggesting this on all occasions, by repeating his proverb : " If they give you the cow, you have to carry the rope."   All we are given is possibilities—to make ourselves one thing or another.   At this instant, for example, you are engaged in listening : decidedly no easy occupation, as you can tell from the fact that if you relax your attention the least bit, your listening will sink into mere hearing ; or a bit more, and your fugitive attention would fail to register the boom of a cannon.

I say, then, that the circumstances offer a magnificent opportunity for a thorough reform of the Spanish state and university.   But the reform of the one and of the other waits to be done *by someone*.   Is there such a one in Spain to-day ? By that I do not mean an individual, of course, one of those mythical creatures usually referred to, by a misapprehension, as a Great Man.   History is not made by one man—however great he may be.   History is not like a sonnet ; nor is it a game of solitaire.   It is made by many people : by groups of people endowed, collectively, with the necessary qualities.

Since I have come here to-day with the intention of talking to you in absolute sincerity ; since, out of loyalty to myself, I am resolved to say my say without mincing words, I cannot disguise my grave doubt whether there exists, on this day, any group capable of achieving the reform of the state, or to limit ourselves to the present theme, the reform of the university.   I say on this day—this fleeting day on which I am speaking.   Within a dozen days, or weeks, this group *can* exist and I hope it will.   Nothing prevents it from being brought together and organized : if I stress so emphatically that we lack such a group to-day, it is with the sole purpose of contributing to its realization to-morrow.

But you will say : " How can you doubt that a group exists, capable of effecting the reform ?   Once it is admitted that a thing is feasible, all that is necessary is the will to do it.   And here are we, fairly clamouring for the reform of the university. There can be no doubt whether the group exists."

Certainly, certainly.   To accomplish a thing which is possible, all you need is the will to do it.   But everything depends on how fully the sense of this easy word is understood.   It is easy to say and even to think that you are resolved upon something ; but it is extremely difficult to be resolved in the true sense.

For this means resolving upon all the things which are necessary as intermediate steps ; it means, for one thing, providing ourselves with the qualities that are requisite for the undertaking. Anything short of this is no real resolution, it is simply wishing. You rinse your imagination in the idea, you work yourself into a voluptuous excitement over it, and you spend your force in a vague effervescence of enthusiasm.   In his *Philosophy of Universal History*, Hegel asserts that passion, without doubt, is responsible for all the significant accomplishments in history ; but—he qualifies—*cool passion*.   When passion is simply a frenzy of turbulent emotion, it is of no use at all.   Anyone could be passionate, that way.   But it is not so easy to maintain that sort of fire which is both critical and creative, that incandescence so supplied with thermal energy that it will not be cooled when the two coldest things in the world come to lodge within it : cool logic and an iron will.   The vulgar, false, impotent sort of passion shrinks in terror from the proximity of reflective thought, for it senses that at such a chilly contact it will be frozen out of existence.   Hence the symptom of high creative passion is that it seeks to complete itself by uniting with the cooler virtues ; that it admits of reflective criticism, without losing its creative energy.   It is fire supported with the constancy of clear understanding and a calm will.

This kind of resolute, clear-seeing will is what I do not find to-day, even at a formative stage, in any group of Spaniards— including yourselves.   And without it, we shall await in vain the execution of a reform, a work of construction and creation.

The root of Spain's troubles, whether in the state or the

university, may be given the most various names ; but if you seek the very tip of the root, out of which all the rest arises and emerges, you encounter a fact which only one word can adequately describe : slovenliness.[1] It penetrates our whole national life from top to bottom, directing, inspiring its actions. The state is slovenly in its dealings with the citizen, permitting him, on occasion, to evade compliance with its laws ; or vice versa, the state itself applies the laws fraudulently and makes them a means of deceiving the citizen. Some day the story will be told, for instance, of what the government did on the authority of that famous law passed during the emergences of the World War, called the " Law of Subsistences ". Things you would consider a far cry from any question of subsistence were perpetrated under the title of this law. Everyone knows what use the governors of provinces have made, for decades, of the Law of Associations. Just ask about that for yourselves, among the labour unions in the provinces. But it is not my intention now to present pathetic cases of this shabby deportment of the state. I am not here to talk politics, and moreover if I were, I should not be pathetic about it. My purpose is to make clear to you what constitutes this fundamental ailment of Spain and the Spaniard, which I call slovenliness. For it is of no use to rant and declaim, after the fashion of public orations, that this conduct of the government is a crime, an intolerable abuse, a betrayal of public trust. It is all that, of course ; but so meanly, so stupidly, so habitually —so far from any compensating profit to the government—that one feels ashamed to call it crime. To tell the truth, while it is crime in the juridical sense, it is not crime as a psychological fact —as a historical reality. Crime is something violent and terrible, and in this regard, respectable : this is no crime, but something inferior to crime. It is, in a word, slovenliness, the lack of all decorum, of all self-respect, of all decency in the state's manner of performing its peculiarly delicate function.

I do not mean by this that in Spain crimes are not committed. But I do deny that crimes are the bulk, or the worst, of Spain's trouble. For crimes, when they are really that, provoke a reaction, before very long, to cure the ailment. Slovenliness on the contrary grows accustomed to its own presence ; it finds itself pleasantly comfortable, and tends to spread and perpetuate itself. Thus it permeates everything in Spain, from the state and its official acts, to the life of the family and the very grimace

[1] EDITOR's NOTE : One would like a slightly milder word to render *la chabacanería*.

of the individual. In our university faculty meetings, the atmosphere is heavy with this slovenliness ; and to walk through these halls, even on ordinary days, and hear the hullabaloo and see the gesticulations of you students, is to breathe an atmosphere so thick with slovenliness that it chokes.[1]

But the full meaning of a concept never becomes clear until it is confronted with its opposite, as for example up and down, more and less, etc. Every idea has its antagonist ; in the combat between the two, their profile is delineated. What is the opposite of slovenliness ? I shall use a word with which you are very familiar, since it belongs to the vocabulary of sports. The opposite of slovenliness is *to be in form*. You people well know the tremendous difference there is between an athlete when he is *in form*, and the same man when he is out of form. The difference in what he is able to do is every bit as striking as if he were two entirely different people. But this *form* is a thing that has to be acquired. In order to achieve it, the individual must first go off by himself and concentrate upon his own development : he has to go into training, and give up many things, in the determination to surpass himself, to be more alert, tense, supple. There is nothing that is indifferent to him, for every little thing either is favourable to his form, or else pulls it down, and with this in mind he goes out for one thing and avoids the other. Briefly, to be in form means never indulging in any dissipation whatever. And that indulgence of oneself—your " let it go anyhow ", " it's all the same ", " a bit more or less ", " what of it ? "—that is slovenliness.

Just as individuals, groups too may be in form or out of form, and it is evident in history that the only groups which have ever done anything are those which have achieved *form* : compact, perfectly organized groups, in which every member knows that the others will not fail him at the crucial point, so that the whole body may move swiftly in any direction without losing its balance or losing its head—as the abbé Fernando Galiani said of the Society of the Jesuits in the eigtheenth century, when that Order was in form, " It is a sword with its hilt in Rome and its point everywhere." But a group does not acquire this *form* unless it has disciplined itself, and continues to discipline itself ; unless it sees with perfect clarity what it proposes to do.

---

[1] AUTHOR'S NOTE : For a number of years I have had to find a room outside the university buildings, because the habitual shouting of our precious students, standing around in the halls, makes it impossible to hear oneself talk in the classrooms.

And it cannot see clearly unless the purpose it sees is clear, well thought out, cogent, and as complete as the situation warrants

All this is what I was referring to earlier. I doubt, then, whether there exists in Spain, at the present moment a group which is *in form* for the reforming of the state or of the university. And if it is not *in form*, all that may be attempted without the necessary qualities will come to nothing. It is obvious, in as much as slovenliness is the root of the evil, that a reform which is slovenly itself will not mend matters appreciably. You have seen for yourselves a petulant effort to reform the country, on the part of a group of people who had not given a moment's thought to the question of first providing themselves with the minimum of necessary equipment. Such had been the Dictatorship.[1] All it has achieved, despite the extraordinary opportunity that offered itself, has been to carry our national slovenliness to the point of madness.

Let it be understood that I have not come here to advise you against taking part in the public affairs of Spain, or against petitioning, and even insisting upon, the reform of the university. On the contrary : I urge you to do all this ; but do it seriously —do it *in form*. Otherwise, the future can be told now, with perfect assurance. If you attempt to take a part in public life without the proper preparation, this is what will happen. Since activity in public affairs means trying to influence the great mass of the public, and you are not a powerful, articulated body but merely a little formless mass, then the mechanics of history, identical at this point with the laws of physics, will simply follow its inexorable course. The larger mass will crush the smaller.

To exert influence upon a mass, you must be something other than a mass yourselves : a live force, or in other words, a group *in form*.

If I could see in you the determination to put yourselves in form—ah !—then, my friends, I should not be afflicted with this deficiency of faith.

I should believe it all to be possible, indeed imminent. Contrary to a general belief, history may advance by jumps, and not always by gradual change. It was the characteristic error of the past century to count upon gradual evolution, and to presume that every whole achievement in history was produced by means of a very gradual preparation. It was a surprise when

---

[1] EDITOR'S NOTE : The dictatorship had begun under Primo de Rivera in 1923, and was to last until the establishment of the Republic in 1931.

facts showed, clearly and undeniably, that in biology and in the spiritual world alike, spontaneous realities could emerge suddenly and in a sense without preparation.

To cite a symbolic case, let me recall to you how stupefied the historians were in the last century, when the fact was established that the highest, classical civilization of the Egyptians— the marvellous culture of the Pyramids—was without predecessors. It caused great astonishment to find that this most exquisite flourishing in the whole course of the Nile valley civilization appeared at the threshold of history—at the dawn of historic times. It had been supposed that excavation would reveal, under the land of the Pyramids, some vestiges of a less perfect culture, in progress towards that mature perfection. Great was the surprise when the archaeologists struck the remains, almost immediately under the pyramids, of a neolithic civilization. Which is to say that almost without transition, man had advanced from the chipped stone to the classic stone.[1]

No ; history proceeds very often by jumps. These jumps, in which tremendous distances may be covered, are called generations. A generation *in form* can accomplish what centuries failed to achieve without form. And there, my young friends, lies a challenge.

[1] Editor's Note : Though later evidence indicates a longer and more significant epoch of transition, the case still illustrates the possibility of rapid social evolution.

CHAPTER II

THE FUNDAMENTAL QUESTION

[1] The reform of higher education cannot be limited, nor can even its main features be limited, to the correction of abuses. Reform is always the creation of new usages. Abuses are always of minor importance. For either they are abuses in the most natural sense of the word, namely, isolated, infrequent cases of departure from usage ; or else they are so frequent and customary, so persistent and so generally tolerated, that they are no longer to be called abuses. In the first case, they will presumably be corrected automatically ; in the second case, it would be futile to correct them, for their frequency and acceptance indicate that they are not exceptions to a rule, but manifestations of usages which are bad. It is something in the usage, the policy, and not the breach of it, which needs our attention.

Any reform movement which is limited to correcting slovenly or slipshod abuses in our university will lead inevitably to a reform which is equally slovenly.

What matters is usage. I can go further : a clear symptom that the usages constituting an institution are sound is the ability to withstand a good dose of abuses without serious harm, as a healthy man bears up under stress that would break a weakling. But an institution cannot be built of wholesome usage, until its precise mission has been determined. An institution is a machine in that its whole structure and functioning must be devised in view of the service it is expected to perform. In other words, the root of university reform is a complete formulation of its purpose. Any alteration, or touching up, or adjustment about this house of ours, unless it starts by reviewing the problem of its mission—clearly, decisively, truthfully—will be love's labour lost.

Through their failure to do this, all the improvements attempted hitherto, motivated in some cases by excellent intentions, including the projects worked out some years ago by the university faculty itself, have inevitably come to nought. They will never achieve the one thing which is both sufficient and requisite for any being—individual or collective—to live to the

[1] EDITOR'S NOTE : The first three paragraphs of Chapter II have here been omitted. In them Ortega recapitulates Chapter I, and complains of the hall in which he had read that chapter. This is the only omission made in the present translation.

full of its powers : namely, that its life be the true, authentic fulfilment of its powers, and not some falsification of this inexorable destiny, imposed upon it by our stubborn and arbitrary preferences. The best attempts of the last fifteen years—not to speak of the worst—instead of putting the question squarely, " What is a university for, and what must it consequently be ? " have done the thing that was easiest and most sterile. They have looked about to see what is done in the universities of other peoples.

I do not criticize our informing ourselves by observing an exemplary neighbour ; on the contrary, that is necessary. But such observation cannot excuse us from the labour of determining our destiny for ourselves. By this I do not mean any quest after " racial purity " and all that nonsense. Even if we were all—men or nations—identical with one another, imitation would still be fatal. For in imitating, we evade that creative exertion of labouring at a problem, from which we can learn the real nature, including the limits and the defects, of the solution we borrow. There is no question here of " racial purity ", which is, in Spain anyway, as common as hayseeds. It is immaterial whether we come to the same conclusions and the same forms as other countries ; what matters is that we arrive by our own legs, after a personal combat with the fundamental question at issue.

The reasoning of our best attempts so far has been fallacious : British life has been, and is, a marvel ; *therefore* the British secondary schools must be exemplary, *since* out of them British life has grown. German science is prodigious ; *therefore* the German university is a model institution, *because* it engendered the prodigy. So let us imitate the British secondary schools and the German higher education.

The error stems directly from the nineteenth century as a whole. The English rout Napoleon I : " The battle of Waterloo was won on the playing fields of Eton." Bismarck crushes Napoleon III : " The war of 1870 is the victory of the Prussian schoolmaster and the German professor."

These clichés rest upon a fundamental error which we shall simply have to get out of our heads. It consists in supposing that nations are great *because* their schools are good—elementary, secondary, or higher. It is the residue of a pious " idealism " of the past century. It ascribes to the school a force which it neither has nor can have. That century, in order to feel enthusiasm for a thing, or even just to esteem it especially, found it necessary to exaggerate the thing to heroic proportions. Certainly *when* a nation is great, so will be its schools. There is no great nation without great schools. But the same holds for its religion, its statesmanship, its economy, and a thousand other things. A nation's greatness is the integration of many elements. If a people is bad politically, it is vain to expect anything at all of the most perfect school system. In such a case schools are for the few, who live apart and estranged from the rest of the country. Perhaps some day these educated few may influence the collective life of their country, and succeed in improving the whole national school system.

Principle of education : the school, when it is truly a functional organ of the nation, depends far more on the atmosphere of national culture in which it is immersed than it does on the pedagogical atmosphere created artificially within it. A condition of equilibrium between this inward and outward pressure is essential to produce a good school.

Consequence : even granting that English secondary education and German higher education are perfect, they would not be transferable, for the institutions are only a part of a larger entity. Their being, in its totality, is nothing less than the whole nation which created and maintains them.

Furthermore, the short-circuited reasoning I have described prevented its victims from looking squarely at these model schools and seeing what they are within themselves, purely as institutional structures. The framework was confused with the ambient air of English life, or German thought. Now in as much as neither English life nor German thought can be transported here but, at best, only the disengaged institutional structures, it is quite important that we see what these actually are, apart from those virtues which enveloped and pervaded them in their native countries.

Then one sees that the German university is, as an institution, a rather deplorable object. If German science had been dependent for its nourishment on the forces of the university, as an institution, that science would be of very small account. Fortunately an atmosphere of free inquiry has combined with the German's natural talent and disposition for science to outweigh the glaring imperfections of the German university. I am not well acquainted with English secondary education ; but what I can discern of it leads me to think that there too the institutional structure is very defective.

But there is no need of my personal opinions. It is a fact, that secondary education in England and the university in Germany are undergoing a crisis. Fundamental criticism of the latter by the first Prussian Minister of Education since the founding of the Republic : Becker. The discussion which has ensued.[1]

Because they have been willing to imitate and to evade thinking through the questions for themselves, our best professors live in all respects in a spirit fifteen or twenty years behind the times, except that they are up to date in the details of their fields. And this is the tragic lag behindhand, which is the fate of people who try to save themselves the effort of being authentic and forming their own convictions. The number of years comprising this lag is not a matter of chance. All the creation of history—in science, in politics—arises out of a certain pervading state of mind, or " spirit of the times ". This state of mind changes at rhythmic intervals : the interval of the generation.[2] Out of the spirit of a generation come ideas, evaluations, and so on. The person who imitates these must wait until they have been formulated ; or in other words, until the preceding generation has finished its work. Then he adopts its principles, at the time when they are beginning to decline, and a new generation is already making its reform, inaugurating the régime of a new spirit. Each generation struggles for fifteen years to establish itself, and its synthesis holds together another fifteen years—inevitable anachronism of an imitative, unauthentic people.

Let us look abroad for information. But not for a model.

There is no evading the fundamental question, then : What is the mission of the university ?

To determine what the mission of the university is, let us try first to define what the university actually means to-day, in Spain and elsewhere. Whatever may be the differences in status, all

[1] EDITOR'S NOTE : See p. 49 and note. For the explanation of Ortega's unfinished sentences see his dedication, p. 26 and the Introduction, page 8.

[2] EDITOR'S NOTE : Ortega has elaborated " The Concept of the Generation " in *The Modern Theme*, Chapter I and ff. For the background of the concept, see the résumé and brief bibliography in Christian Sénéchal, *Les grands courants de la littérature française contemporaine*, Paris : Malfère (1933), pp. 419–21 ; the introduction of Bopp and Paulhan to Albert Thibaudet, *Histoire de la littérature française de 1789 à nos jours*, Paris : Stock (1937) ; and also Sainte-Beuve's observation concerning individual literary production, in *Nouveaux lundis*, III, art. " Chateaubriand ", part II (1862) : " Quinze ans d'ordinaire font une carrière ; il est donné à quelques-uns de la doubler, d'en recommencer ou même d'en remplir une seconde."

the universities of Europe have some general characteristics in common.[1]

We meet the fact, first of all, that the university is the institution in which higher education is imparted to almost all those who receive any. " Almost," because there are also the specialized schools, whose separate existence gives rise to a problem likewise separate. Having made this exception, we may lay it aside and work with the practical generalization, that the people who receive higher education receive it in the university. But then we find ourselves face to face with another limitation more important than that of the specialized schools. All those who receive higher education are not all those who could and should receive it ; they are only the children of the well-to-do classes. The university represents a privilege difficult to justify or defend. Theme : the working class in the university —a theme as yet intact. For two reasons. First, if one believes it is right, as I do, to offer the knowledge of the university to the working man, it is because one considers this knowledge valuable

---

[1] AUTHOR'S NOTE : It is usual, for example, to exaggerate the differences between the English and continental universities, neglecting the fact that the greatest differences are to be laid not to the universities themselves, but to the very extraordinary English character. What should be compared between countries is the tendencies which mark the evolution of their universities—not the degree, naturally variable, in which the tendencies have progressed. Thus, the conservatism of the English has caused them to maintain appearances, in their higher institutions, which they themselves recognize to be irrelevant, and which, indeed, they value as mere fictions quite incidental to the vital reality of British university life. It would seem ridiculous for someone to presume to limit the free will of the Englishman, and censure him for indulging, if he could and wanted to, in the luxury of consciously perpetuating these fictions. But it would be just as naïve to take these figments seriously, and suppose that the Englishman deludes himself about their fictitious character. The studies I have read on the English university fall invariably into the subtle snare of English irony. They fail to notice that if England preserves the non-professional *aspect* of the university, like the wig of the magistrate, it is not through any obstinate belief that these are actualities, but precisely *because* they are antiquated and superfluous. Otherwise they could not provide the luxury, the diversion, the occasion for awe, and other values which the Englishman seeks in these mere appearances. Beneath the quaint peruke, the justice is modern to the minute ; and beneath its nonprofessional aspect, the English university has become, in the last forty years, as professionalized as any other.
It is likewise not of the slightest importance for our central theme—the mission of the university—that the English universities are not institutions of the state. While this fact is of great importance for the life and history of the English people, it does not prevent their universities from functioning essentially in the same way as the state-maintained universities of the continent. In the last analysis it would turn out that even in England the universities are institutions of the state ; only the Englishman has an entirely different conception of the state from the continental idea of it. To sum up the point I wish to make : first, the enormous differences which exist between the universities of the various nations are not so much concerned with the universities proper as with the nations themselves ; and second, the most striking fact in the last forty years is a convergent movement of all the universities of Europe that is tending to make them all homogeneous.

and desirable. The problem of universalizing the university rests upon the previous determination of what the higher learning and instruction are to be. And second, the process of making the university accessible to the working man is only in small part the concern of the university ; it is almost wholly the business of the state. Only a great reform of our state will make our university effective. Failure of all the attempts made so far, such as " university extension ", etc.[1]

The important thing at this point is to bear well in mind that all the people who receive higher education receive it in the university. If a greater number should receive it to-morrow than at present, so much the better for the force of the argument which follows.

Of what does this higher instruction consist, which is offered in the university to the vast legion of youth ? It consists of two things :

(A) The teaching of the learned professions.

(B) Scientific research and the preparation of future investigators.

The university teaches people to be doctors, pharmacists, lawyers, judges, economists, public servants, teachers of the sciences and the humanities in secondary schools, and so on.

In the second place, science itself is cultivated in the university, through research and the transmission of its methods. In Spain, this function of creative science, and of creating scientists, is at a minimum ; not by reason of any defect of the university, nor because the university considers that such activities are not its mission, but on account of the notorious lack of scientific callings and aptitude for research which marks our race. No doubt if science were abundantly carried on in Spain, it would be in the university by preference, as is more or less the case in the other countries. Let this point serve as an example, and save us the repetition of the same principle at every step : the obstinate backwardness of Spain in intellectual activity entails the result that we find here in a state of germination or mere tendency what

---

[1] EDITOR'S NOTE : It should be noted that after half a century of growth, university extension in the United States has become an important agency for the training of people who must meanwhile earn their living. The cultural education of the working man is still admittedly deficient ; but this is due rather to our poor understanding of the objective than to a lack of well-intentioned agencies. Organizations and institutions interested in the education of the working man are too numerous to need mention. Among the oldest are the British " Workers' Educational Association ", and Ruskin College in Oxford (founded 1899). For the explanation of Ortega's unfinished sentences see his dedication, p. 26 and the Introduction, page 8.

appears elsewhere in its full development. For the purpose of stating the university problem in its basic form, these differences of degree are immaterial. It is sufficient that all the reforms of recent years clearly evince the intention to increase the research activities of our universities and the training of scientists : in short, to orient the entire institution in this direction. Commonplace and deceptive objections may be advanced on the other side. It is, however, notorious that our best professors, those who have the most influence in the course of the attempted reforms, believe that our university should vie with the foreign universities. And that is enough.

The higher education consists, then, of professionalism and research. Without attacking the subject now, let us note in passing that it is surprising to find two such disparate tasks joined, fused together. For there can be no doubt about this : to be a lawyer, a judge, a doctor, a druggist, a teacher of Latin or history in a secondary school, is very different from being a jurist, a physiologist, a biochemist, a philologist, etc. The former are engaged in practical professions ; the latter in purely scientific occupations. Furthermore, society needs many doctors, pharmacists, teachers ; but it needs only a restricted number of scientists.[1] If we really needed many of these it would be a catastrophe, since a true calling for science is extremely rare. It is surprising, then, to find mixed together the professional instruction which is for all, and research which is for a very few. But let us put this matter aside for a few moments. Is the higher education nothing more than professionalism and research ? At first sight we discover nothing else. But if we scrutinize the programmes of instruction more closely, we discover that the student is nearly always required, apart from his professional apprenticeship and his research, to take some courses of a general character—philosophy, history.

It takes no great acumen to recognize in this requirement the last, miserable residue of something more imposing and more meaningful. The symptom that something is a residue— whether in biology or in history—is that we do not perceive why it is with us. In its present form, it serves no end at all ; one must trace it back to some other age of its evolution in order to find whole and active what exists to-day only as a

---

[1] AUTHOR'S NOTE : This number needs to be greater than has been attained at present ; but even so, incomparably smaller than the number in the other professions.

residual stump.[1] The justification which is advanced to-day,
in support of that ancient precept of higher education, is rather
vague. The student ought, it is said, to receive something of
" general culture ".

" General culture." The absurdity of the term, its
Philistinism, betrays its insincerity. " Culture," referring to the
human mind and not to stock or crops, cannot be anything else
but general. There is no being " cultured " in physics or mathematics. That would mean simply to be *learned* in a particular
subject. The usage of the expression " general culture " shows
an underlying notion that the student ought to be given some
ornamental knowledge, which in some way is to educate his
moral character or his intellect. For so vague a purpose, one
discipline is as good as another, among those that are more or
less indefinite and not so technical—like philosophy, or history,
or sociology !

But the fact is that if we go back to the medieval epoch in
which the university was created, we see clearly that the relic
before us is the humble remains of what then constituted higher
education, proper and entire.

The medieval university does no research.[2] It is very little
concerned with professions. All is " *general culture* "—theology,
philosophy, " arts." [3]

But what is called " general culture " to-day was something
very different for the Middle Ages. It was not an ornament
for the mind or a training of the character. It was, on the
contrary, the system of ideas, concerning the world and humanity,
which the man of that time possessed. It was, consequently, the
repertory of convictions which became the effective guide of his
existence.

Life is a chaos, a tangled and confused jungle in which man
is lost. But his mind reacts against the sensation of bewilder-

---

[1] AUTHOR'S NOTE : Imagine for a moment the conditions of primitive life. One
of its constant characteristics is the lack of personal security. It is perilous for two
persons to approach each other, for everyone goes about armed. Hence this act
has to be safeguarded by customs and ceremonies which give assurance that weapons
have been left behind, and that the hand is not going to reach suddenly for one that
is hidden. For this purpose, the best procedure is for each man, upon approaching,
to grasp the hand of the other—the killing hand, which is normally the right hand.
Such is the origin and purpose of our salute by shaking hands, which in the present
times, remote from that type of life, is an incomprehensible relic.

[2] AUTHOR'S NOTE : Which does not mean that no research was done in the Middle
Ages.

[3] EDITOR'S NOTE : The exaggeration here does not essentially damage Sr. Ortega's
thesis that the modern university should teach a kind of " culture " which this reference to the Middle Ages helps to describe.

ment : he labours to find " roads ", " ways " through the woods,[1] in the form of clear, firm ideas concerning the universe, positive convictions about the nature of things.   The ensemble, or system, of these ideas, is culture in the true sense of the term ; it is precisely the opposite of external ornament.   Culture is what saves human life from being a mere disaster ; it is what enables man to live a life which is something above meaningless tragedy or inward disgrace.

We cannot live on the human level without ideas. Upon them depends what we do.   Living is nothing more or less than doing one thing instead of another.   Hence the oldest book of India : " Our acts follow our thoughts as the wheel of the cart follows the hoof of the ox."   In this sense—which by itself implies no intellectualistic doctrine [2]—we *are* our ideas.

Gideon, in this case exceptionally profound, would make it clear that man is always born into a specific period.   That is, he is called to live his life at some definite stage in the unfolding of human destinies.   A man belongs to a generation ; he is of one substance with it.   And each generation takes its place not in some chance location, but directly and squarely upon the preceding one.   This comes to mean that man lives, perforce, at *the level of his time*,[3] and more particularly, at *the level of the ideas of his time.*

Culture is the *vital* system of ideas of a period.   It makes not a particle of difference whether these ideas, or convictions, lie partly or wholly in the province of science.   Culture is not science.   It is characteristic of our present culture that a great part of its content proceeds out of science ; but in other cultures this has not been the case, nor is it decreed anywhere that in ours it will always be so to the same degree as at present.

Compared with the medieval university, the contemporary university has developed the mere seed of professional instruction into an enormous activity ; it has added the function of research ; and it has abandoned almost entirely the teaching or transmission of culture.

It is evident that the change has been pernicious.   Europe to-day is taking its sinister consequences.   The convulsive situation in Europe at the present moment is due to the fact that

---

[1] AUTHOR'S NOTE : Whence there arises at the beginning of all cultures a term expressing " road " in this sense : the *hodos* and *methodos* of the Greeks, the *tao* and *te* of the Chinese, the *path* and *vehicle* of India.

[2] AUTHOR'S NOTE : Our ideas or convictions may well be unintellectualistic, as mine are, and in general, the ideas of our age.

[3] AUTHOR'S NOTE : For the concept of " the height of the times ", see *The Revolt of the Masses.*

the average Englishman, the average Frenchman, the average German are *uncultured* : they are ignorant of the essential system of ideas concerning the world and man, which belong to our time. This average person is the new barbarian, a laggard behind the contemporary civilization, archaic and primitive in contrast with his problems, which are grimly, relentlessly modern.[1] This new barbarian is above all the professional man, more learned than ever before, but at the same time more uncultured —the engineer, the physician, the lawyer, the scientist.

The blame for this unpredicted barbarity, this radical and tragic anachronism, rests primarily with the pretentious nineteenth-century university of all countries. If this institution should by chance be torn to bits in the frenzy of a barbarous revolution, it would not have the feeblest reason to complain. When one has examined the matter, he must needs come to the conclusion that the guilt of the universities is not compensated for by the prodigious and brilliant service which they have undeniably rendered to science. Let us not be the dupes of science. For if science is the grandest creation of man, it is made possible, after all, by human life. A crime perpetrated against the fundamental conditions of human life cannot be atoned for through science.

The harm is so ingrained that I shall barely be understood by the generation anterior to the one I am addressing.

In the book of a Chinese thinker who lived in the fourth century B.C., Chuang-tsu, certain symbolic characters are conversing together, and one of them, called the God of the Northern Sea, asks, " How shall I talk of the sea to the frog, if he has never left his pond ? How shall I talk of the frost to the bird of the summer land, if it has never left the land of its birth ? How shall I talk of life with the sage, if he is the prisoner of his doctrine ? "

Society needs good professional men—judges, doctors, engineers—and therefore the university is prepared to furnish professional training. But society needs before this, and more than this, to be assured that the capacity is developed for another kind of profession, the profession of governing. In every society someone governs, whether a group or a class, few people or many. By " governing " I mean not so much the legal exercise of authority as a diffuse pressure, or influence, exerted upon the

[1] AUTHOR'S NOTE : The analysis of this serious situation is presented in *The Revolt of the Masses.*

body politic. To-day, the societies in Europe are governed by the bourgeois classes, the majority of whom are composed of professional men.   It is of the first importance to these societies, therefore, that these professional people, aside from their several professions, possess the power to make their lives a vital influence, in harmony with the height of their times.   Hence it is imperative to set up once more, in the university, the teaching of the culture, the system of vital ideas, which the age has attained.   This is the basic function of the university.   This is what the university must be, above all else.

If the working man should become the governing man to-morrow, the problem remains the same : he must govern in accordance with the height of the times—otherwise his regime will be supplanted.[1]

When one considers that the European countries have deemed it admissible to grant professional titles and prestige to magistrates and doctors without making sure that these men have a clear idea, for example, of the physical conception we now have of the world, and an equally clear idea of the character and limitations of the marvellous science by which that concept had been attained —we need not be surprised that affairs have come to such a pass in Europe.   At a juncture like this, let us not bandy about fine phrases.   The vague desire for a vague culture, I repeat, will lead us nowhere.   Physics, and its method, is one of the great essential instruments of the modern mind.   Into that science have gone four centuries of intellectual discipline, and its doctrine is intimately connected with the cultured man's concept of God and society, of matter and that which is not matter, together with all the other essentials for an enlightened life.   Of course, one can do without that science and be neither disgraced nor condemned —in certain situations : if one is a humble shepherd in the hills, or a serf attached to the soil, or a manual labourer enslaved to the machine.   But the gentleman who professes to be a doctor, or magistrate, or general, or philologist, or bishop—that is, a person who belongs to the directive class of society—if he is ignorant of what the physical cosmos is to-day for the European man, is a perfect barbarian, however well he may know his laws, or his medicines, or his Holy Fathers.   And I should say the same of the person who has not a decently coherent picture of the great

---

[1] AUTHOR'S NOTE : Since in actual practice the working man does govern, sharing that function with the middle class, it is urgent that the university education be extended to him.

movements of history which have brought Humanity to its present parting of the ways (for ours is a day of crucial situations). And I should say the same again of the person who has no definite idea of how speculative philosophy conceives to-day its perpetual essay to formulate a plan of the universe ; or how biology endeavours to interpret the fundamental facts of organic life.

For the moment, let us not obscure this simple, evident proposition, by raising the question of how a lawyer, without preparation in higher mathematics, can understand the idea of twentieth-century physics. We shall deal with that question later. For now, let us simply admit into our minds, as we must, the light which proceeds from this observation. The man who does not possess the concept of physics (not the science of physics proper, but the vital idea of the world which it has created), and the concept afforded by history and by biology, and the scheme of speculative philosophy, is not an educated man. Unless he should happen to be endowed with exceptional qualities, it is extremely unlikely that such a man will be, in the fullest sense, a good doctor, a good judge, or a good technical expert. But it is certain that all the other things he does in life, including parts of his profession itself which transcend its proper academic boundaries, will turn out unfortunately. His political ideas and actions will be inept ; his affairs of the heart, beginning with the type of woman he will prefer, will be crude and ridiculous ; he will bring to his family life an atmosphere of unreality and cramped narrowness, which will warp the upbringing of his children ; and outside, with his friends, he will emit thoughts that are monstrosities, and opinions that are a torrent of drivel and bluff.

There is no other way : to move with assurance in the tangle of life, one must be cultivated, one must know the topography —the " ways " and " methods ". One must have an idea of the time and place in which he lives : in a word, the " culture " of the age. Now then, this culture is either received, or else it is invented. He who exposes himself to the labour of inventing it for himself, accomplishing alone what thirty centuries of humanity have already accomplished, is the only man who has the right to deny the proposition that the university must undertake to impart culture. But the unfortunate truth is that this lone person, who could oppose my thesis, would have to be a madman !

Civilization has had to await the beginning of the twentieth century, to see the astounding spectacle of how brutal, how

stupid, and yet how aggressive is the man learned in one thing
and fundamentally ignorant of all else.[1] Professionalism and
specialism, through insufficient counterbalancing, have smashed
the European man in pieces ; and he is consequently missing at
all the points where he claims to be, and is badly needed. The
engineer possesses engineering ; but that is just one piece, one
dimension of the European man : the whole man is not to be
found in this fragment called " engineer ". And so in the rest
of the cases. When one says that " Europe is broken in pieces ",
thinking to use a baroque and exaggerated expression, he says
more truth than he suspects. Indeed, the crumbling away of
Europe which we are witnessing is the result of the invisible
fragmentation that the European man has progressively
undergone.[2]

The great task immediately before us is something like a
jigsaw puzzle : we have to reassemble out of scattered pieces—
disiecta membra—a complete living organism, the European man.
What we must achieve is that every individual, or (not to be
Utopian) many individuals, should each succeed in constituting
the type of the whole man in its entirety. What force can bring
this about, if it is not the university ?

Then there are no two ways about it. The university must
add this other function, huge as it is, to the list of those it already
attempts to accomplish.

For that matter, outside Spain a movement is making itself
felt with great vigour, to orient higher education towards the
teaching of culture, or the transmission to the newer generation
of the system of ideas concerning the world and man which has
reached its maturity with the passing generation.

We come to the conclusion therefore that the university's
teaching comprises these three functions :

I.   The transmission of culture.
II. The teaching of the professions.
III. Scientific research and the training of new scientists.

Have we thus answered our question, What is the mission of
the university ? By no means ! we have only massed together

---

[1] AUTHOR'S NOTE : See the chapter entitled " The barbarism of specialization "
in The Revolt of the Masses.
[2] AUTHOR'S NOTE : The statement is true to such a point that it cannot only be
made thus vaguely, but it can be developed by enumerating the precise phases of
the progressive fragmentation, in the three generations of the past century and th▪
first generation of the twentieth.

what the university of to-day believes to be its business, and a work which, in our judgment, it is not doing but must do. We have prepared the question ; no more than that.

It seems to me unnecessary, or at least incidental, to debate as did the philosopher Scheler and the Minister of Education Becker, a few years ago, over the question whether these functions are to be performed by a single institution or by various institutions.[1] It is vain because in the end all these functions would unite in the person of the student : they would all eventually come to gravitate around his adolescent years, as a common centre.

The question is different. It is this : Even when instruction is limited, as at present, to professional matters and the methods of science, the result is a fabulous profusion of studies. It is impossible even for the better than ordinary student to come anywhere near real success in learning what the university professes to teach him. But institutions exist—they are necessary and they have meaning—because the ordinary man exists. If there were none but extraordinary creatures, it is very probable that there would be no institutions, either educational or political.[2] It is therefore necessary to consider any institution with reference to the man of ordinary endowment. For him it is made, and he must be its unit of measure.

Let us suppose for a moment that in the university, as it is, we find nothing which deserves to be called an abuse. Everything is running smoothly and properly according to what the university professes itself to be. Very well : even then I should say the university of to-day is an abuse in itself, because it is, in itself, a falsehood.

It is so thoroughly impossible for the ordinary student to master what the university tries to teach him, that it has become a part of university life to accept the failure. In other words, it is taken for granted as a regular thing, that what the university attempts to be is a delusion. We accept the falsity of the university's inward life—its very essence is composed of its own falsification. This is the root of the whole trouble (as it always is in life, individual or collective). The original sin stems from

[1] EDITOR'S NOTE : See especially Carl Heinrich Becker (by error " Beeker " in the Spanish editions), *Gedanken zur Hochschulreform*, Leipzig : Quelle u. Meyer, 1919 ; and Max Scheler, " *Innere Widersprüche der deutschen Universitäten*," *Westdeutsche Wochenschrift* 1, 32 : 493–5 ; 33 : 511–12 ; 34 : 524–7 ; 35 : 539–41 ; 36 : 551–3.
[2] AUTHOR'S NOTE : Anarchy is logical when it declares all institutions to be useless and thus pernicious, for it starts with the postulate that every man is extraordinary by birth—i.e. good, prudent, intelligent, and just.

the pretension to be other than one's true self.   It is our privilege
to *try* to be whatever we wish ; but it is vicious to pretend to be
what we are not, and to delude ourselves by growing habituated
to a radically false idea of what we are.   When the habitual
behaviour of a man or an institution is false, the next step is
complete demoralizàtion.   And thence to degeneracy, for it is
not possible for anyone to submit to the falsification of his nature
without losing his self-respect.

That is why Leonardo da Vinci said : " Chi non può quel
che vuol, quel che può voglia "—" Who cannot what he will, let
him will what he can."

This maxim of Leonardo's must guide from the beginning
any real reform of the university.   Only a firm resolution to be
genuine will bear fruit.   And not only the life of the university,
but the whole new life must be fashioned by artisans whose first
thought is *authenticity*.   (Note this, Younger Generation.   Otherwise, you are lost.   In fact you show signs of being lost already.)

An institution, then, which feigns to give and to require what
it cannot, is false and demoralized.   Yet this principle of deceit
is to be found throughout the whole plan and structure of the
present university.

The conclusion seems to me inescapable, that we must turn
the present university upside down, so to speak, and stand it
upon precisely the opposite principle.   Instead of teaching what
ought to be taught, according to some Utopian desire, we must
teach only what *can* be taught ; that is, *what can be learned*.

I shall attempt to develop the implications of this formula.

The problem extends in reality quite beyond the subject of
higher education.   It involves the capital question of education
at all levels.

What has been the great historic advance in pedagogy ?
Beyond doubt, the turn it has taken under the inspiration of
Rousseau, Pestalozzi, Froebel, and German idealism, amounting
to a revolutionary avowal of the obvious.   In education there
are three elemental factors : what is taught (knowledge, wisdom),
and the teacher and the learner.   Yet with peculiar blindness,
education had centred about knowledge and the teacher.   The
learner was no factor in pedagogy.   The innovation of Rousseau
and his successors was simply to shift the centre of gravity of the
science from knowledge and the teacher to the learner, recognizing
that it is the learner and his characteristics which alone can guide
us in our effort to make something organic of education.   Know-

ledge and research have their own structure, which is not applicable to that other activity proposing to impart knowledge. The principle of pedagogy is entirely different from that on which culture and science are built.

But we must go a step further. Rather than lose ourselves in a minute study of the learner's characteristics as a child, as a youth, etc., we are constrained to limit the subject for our present purpose, and consider the child and the youth from a more modest point of view, which is more precise : namely, as a student and apprentice. Then we strike upon the fact that it is not the child as a child, or the youth because of his youth, that obliges us to ply this special profession we call " teaching ". It is something far less complicated, and in fact, very definite and simple.

Let me explain.

CHAPTER III

THE PRINCIPLE OF ECONOMY IN EDUCATION

The science of political economy emerged from the war in much the same shattered state as did the economies of the belligerent nations. There was nothing to do but set about reconstructing this whole body of knowledge from the ground up. Such adventures are as a rule beneficial in the life of a science, for they force it to seek a more solid basis than has been in use, a more general and fundamental principle. And in fact at the present time, political economy is arising from its ruins, for a reason so obvious that it is embarrassing to mention. To wit : that economic *science* necessarily responds to the fundamental principle underlying the economic *activity* of man. Why is it that mankind engages in economic occupations, producing, managing, bartering, saving, appraising, etc. ? For one astonishing reason, and that alone : because many of the things man desires and requires are not to be had in unlimited abundance. If all we need existed in plenty and to spare it would never have occurred to men to fatigue themselves with economic exertion. Air, for example, does not usually give rise to activity we could call economic. Yet as soon as air becomes scarce in some way or other, it immediately occasions economic activity. For example children in a schoolroom need a certain amount of air. If the room is small there is a scarcity of air ; hence an economic problem, ending in an enlarged school which is accordingly more expensive.

Again, even though our planet is rolling in air, so to speak, its air is not all of the same quality. " Pure air " is to be had only at certain places, at certain altitudes, under specific conditions of climate. " Pure air " is scarce. And that simple fact provokes an intense economic activity among the Swiss—hotels, sanatoriums—converting this scarce raw material into health, at so much per day.

This is all astonishingly simple, I repeat ; but it is undeniably true. Scarcity is the basis of economic activity, and indeed the Swedish economist Cassel, some years ago, revised the science of economics by taking as a point of departure the *principle of scarcity.*[1] Einstein has remarked many times that " if perpetual motion existed, there would be no such thing as physics ". Similarly, we may be sure that in Elysium there is no economic activity, and consequently no science of economics.

I am persuaded that an analogous situation has its effect in education. Why does pedagogical activity exist at all ? Why is it an occupation and a preoccupation of man ? To these questions the romantics gave most brilliant, moving, and transcendental answers, in which they drew upon all things human and a good portion of the divine. For their taste, it was always necessary to obscure the bare nature of things with festoons of ornamental foliage, and a touch of melodrama. We, on the contrary—am I not right, young people ?—we are content to accept things for what they are (at least for the time being), and nothing more. We like their bareness. We do not mind cold and inclemency. We know that life is hard, and will be hard. We accept the rigour of it ; we do not try to sophisticate destiny. Because life is hard, it does not seem to us any the less magnificent. On the contrary, if it is hard it is also solid and sturdy. Above all, it is free of any hypocrisy. We value openness in our dealings with things. We like to strip things bare, and when they are thus denuded, to wash them clean as we examine them, and see what they are *in puris naturalibus.*

Man is occupied and preoccupied with education for a reason which is simple, bald, and devoid of glamour : in order to live with assurance and freedom and efficiency, it is necessary to know an enormous number of things, and the child or youth has an extremely limited capacity for learning. That is the reason. If childhood and youth lasted a century apiece, or if the child and the adolescent possessed intelligence and the power of attention practically without limit, the teaching activity would never exist. Even if those appealing, transcendental reasons had never operated at all, mankind would have had to develop that variety of the species known as the teacher.

Scarcity of the capacity to learn is the cardinal principle of education. It is necessary to provide for teaching precisely in proportion as the learner is unable to learn.

Is it not a too striking coincidence that the ferment in education erupted towards the middle of the eighteenth century, and

[1] AUTHOR's NOTE : See Gustav Cassel, *Theoretische Sozialökonomie*, 1921, pp. 3 ff. In part this amounts to a return to some positions of classic economics, as opposed to the economics of the last sixty years.

has continued to increase up to the present ?   Why did this not happen sooner ?   The explanation is simple : it was precisely at that time that the first great flowering of modern culture ripened for harvest.   In a short time, the treasure of active human knowledge became enlarged by a tremendous increment.   Life was entering into the full swing of the new capitalism, which recent inventions had made possible : life was consequently assuming a new and appalling complexity, and it was exacting a greater and greater equipment of technics.   Accordingly, along with the necessity for learning a quantity of things quite beyond the capacity to learn, pedagogy was promptly intensified and expanded to meet the need.

In primitive epochs, on the other hand, there is scarcely such a thing as education.[1]   Why should there be, if there is scarcely any need for it—if the capacity to learn is far ahead of the material to be assimilated ?   The capacity is in excess.   There are but a few branches of knowledge, certain magic formulas and rituals for fabricating the most difficult instruments, like the canoe, or for curing illness and casting out devils.   This is all the subject matter there is.   Since it is so scant, anyone could learn it without applying himself with any special effort.   Hence there arises a peculiar situation, which corroborates my thesis in the most unexpected fashion.   The fact is that education appears among primitive peoples in an inverted form : the vocation of teaching is actually one of concealing.   The sacred formulas are conserved as secrets, and passed on esoterically to a chosen few.   Outsiders would learn them all too readily.   Whence the universal phenomenon of secret rites.

The phenomenon is so persistent that it reappears at any level of civilization, when there arises a particularly novel variety of knowledge, superior in kind to all that has been previously known.   Since the new and enviable knowledge exists at first only in small quantity, it is a valuable kind of property, to be imparted only in jealous secrecy.   Thus it happened with the Pythagorean school's philosophy of precision, and even with so enlightened a philosopher as Plato.   For we have his famous seventh epistle, written with the purpose of protesting against the accusation that he had taught his philosophy to Dionysius of

---

[1] EDITOR'S NOTE : The primitive cultures we are able to observe do of course transmit to their youth considerable knowledge of zoology and anatomy, botany, social usage and even philosophy of the differences in tribal cultures.   But the point remains valid, that primitive cultures are not confronted with our problem of an unmanageable quantity of important knowledge.

Syracuse, as if that were a heinous crime.   All primitive education in which there is little to teach, is esoteric and secretive ; in that respect it is the antithesis of education as we conceive it in our day.

Education comes into being, then, when the knowledge which has to be acquired is out of proportion to the capacity to learn. To-day, more than ever before, the profusion of cultural and technical possessions is such that it threatens to bring a catastrophe upon mankind, in as much as every generation is finding it more nearly impossible to assimilate it.

It is urgent therefore for us to base our science of teaching, its methods and institutions, upon the plain, humble principle that the child or the youth who is to be the learner cannot learn all we should like him to know—the principle of economy in education.

Since it could not be otherwise, this rule has always been in operation where there has been pedagogical activity ; but only because it could not be helped, and hence in a restricted degree. It has never been set up as a principle, perhaps because at first sight it is not dramatic—it does not talk of imposing transcendentals.

The university of to-day, outside Spain even more than within, is a tropical underbrush of subject matters.   If to this we add what we have deemed imperative—the teaching of culture—the verdure threatens to hide the horizon altogether : the horizon of youth which needs to be clear and open, in order that it may expose to view the beckoning glow afar off.   There is no remedy but to rise up against this turgid overgrowth and use the principle of economy like a hatchet.   First of all, a thorough pruning.

The principle of economy not only implies that it is necessary to economize in the subject matter to be offered.   It has a further implication : that the organization of higher education, the construction of the university, must be based upon the student, and not upon the professor or upon knowledge.   The university must be the projection of the student to the scale of an institution. And his two dimensions are, first, what he is—a being of limited learning capacity—and second, what he needs to know in order to live his life.

(The present student movement comprises many ingredients. Out of the conventional ten parts, seven are made up of pure buffoonery.   But the other three are absolutely reasonable and more than justify the whole student agitation. One is the political unrest of the country : the soul of the nation is perturbed. The second is a series of real though incredible abuses on the part of a few professors. And the third, which is the most important and decisive, influences the students without their realizing it. It is the fact that neither they nor anybody in particular, but the times themselves, the present circumstances in education throughout the world, are forcing the university to centre itself once more on the student—to *be* the student, and not the professor, as it was in the heyday of its greatness.[1] The tendencies of the times press on inevitably, though mankind, impelled as it is by them, may be unaware of their presence, and quite unable to define them or give them a name. The students should eliminate the discreditable parts of their activity and emphasize these three, especially the last, for in these they are entirely right.[2])

We must begin, therefore, with the ordinary student, and take as a nucleus of the institution, as its central and basic portion *exclusively* the subject matters which can be required with absolute stringency, i.e. those a good ordinary student can really learn

This, I repeat, is what the university should be, at its very base. Presently we shall see that the university must be, in addition, several other things which are no less important But what is important at this point is not to confuse things : it is to separate carefully from one another the various functions and organs of that imposing institution, the university.

How are we to determine the body of subjects which are to constitute the torso or *minimum* of the curriculum ? By submitting the present conglomeration to two tests :

1. We must pick out that which appears as strictly necessary for the life of the man who is now a student. Life, with

---

[1] EDITOR'S NOTE : This is true of both the Parisian and the Bolognese families of the medieval university. While Paris is said to have had a " magisterial constitution ", as opposed to the " student constitution " of the other family, yet even at Paris the students, through their organization in " nations ", had a responsible part in the maintenance of discipline and morale.

[2] AUTHOR'S NOTE : The concept that the university *is* the student is to be carried out even to the point of affecting its material organization. It is absurd to consider the university, as it has been considered hitherto, the professor's house in which he receives pupils. Rather the contrary : put the students in charge of the house and let the student body constitute the torso of the institution, complemented by the faculties of professors. The maintenance of discipline through beadles gives rise to shameful squabbles, and organizes the students into a rebellious horde. The students are not to blame, but the institution, which is badly planned. The students themselves, properly organized for the purpose, should direct the internal ordering of the university, determine the decorum of usages and manners, impose disciplinary measures, and feel responsible for the morale.

its inexorable requirements, is the criterion that should guide this first stroke of the pruning knife.

2. What remains, having been judged strictly necessary, must be further reduced to what the student can really learn with thoroughness and understanding.

It is not enough that this or that is necessary. When we least expect, the necessary suddenly passes beyond the capabilities of the student. It would be fantastic on our part to rant and rave that it is necessary. Only so much must be taught as can truly be learned. On this point we must be unshakable, though the line of action which issues from it is drastic.

CHAPTER IV

WHAT THE UNIVERSITY MUST BE PRIMARILY : THE UNIVERSITY ; PROFESSION AND SCIENCE

By applying the principles we have discussed, we come to the following propositions :

(A) The university consists, primarily and basically, of the higher education which the ordinary man should receive.

(B) It is necessary to make of this ordinary man, first of all, a cultured person : to put him at the height of the times. It follows then, that the primary function of the university is to teach the great cultural disciplines, namely :

1. The physical scheme of the world (Physics).
2. The fundamental themes of organic life (Biology).
3. The historical process of the human species (History).
4. The structure and functioning of social life (Sociology).
5. The plan of the universe (Philosophy).

(C) It is necessary to make the ordinary man a good professional. Besides his apprenticeship to culture, the university will teach him, by the most economical, direct and efficacious procedures intellect can devise, to be a good doctor, a good judge, a good teacher of mathematics or of history. The specific character of this professional teaching must be set aside, however, for fuller discussion.

(D) There is no cogent reason why the ordinary man need or ought to be a scientist. Scandalous consequence : science in the true sense, i.e. scientific investigation, has no place in any direct, constituent capacity among the primary functions of the university. It is something independent. In what sense the university is inseparable from science, and must be in addition a place of scientific research, is a question we shall treat further on.

No doubt this heretical opinion will call down on itself the deluge of inanities which always threatens from the horizon, like a teeming cloud. I realize that there are serious objections against this thesis of mine ; but before these are advanced, we shall see erupting that volcano of commonplaces which every man becomes when he speaks on a question he has not thought out beforehand.

The plan of a university which I am expounding requires

that you indulgently dispose your mind to distinguish three things, each quite different from the others : namely science, culture, and learned profession. You must renounce that restful light in which all cats are grey.

First let us differentiate between profession and science. Science is not just whatever you will. Obviously, it is not science to buy yourself a microscope or to throw together a laboratory. But *neither is it science to expound, or learn, the content of a science.* In its proper and authentic sense, science is exclusively investigation : the posing of problems, working at them, and arriving at their solution. From the moment a solution is reached, all that may subsequently be done with the solution is not science.[1] And that is why it is not science to learn or teach a science, or to apply and appropriate science. It may well be best—with what reservations we shall presently see—for the man entrusted with the teaching of a science to be a scientist at the same time. But that is not absolutely necessary, and as a matter of fact there have been and are prodigious teachers of the sciences who are not investigators, i.e. scientists. It is sufficient that they *know* their science. But to know is not to investigate. To investigate is to discover a truth, or inversely, to demonstrate an error. To know means to assimilate a truth into one's consciousness, to possess a fact after it has been attained and secured.

At the beginnings of science, in Greece, when there was yet little science to be had ready made, men hardly ran the same risk of confusing it with things which are not science. The words they used to designate science exposed its identity with inquiry, creative work, investigation. Even the contemporaries of Plato and Aristotle lacked any term to match exactly—including its equivocalness—the modern word ' science." They spoke of *historia, exetasis, philosophia*, which mean, with one nuance or another, " a learning by inquiry," " a searching out," and " a systematic treatment of a subject, or scientific investigation " —but not " possession of knowledge." The name *philo-sophia* arose, comparatively late, from the effort to distinguish from the usual learning that novel activity which was not to *be learned,* but to *seek* knowledge.[2]

[1] AUTHOR'S NOTE : Except to question it afresh, to convert it back to a problem by criticizing it, and hence to repeat the cycle of scientific investigation.

[2] AUTHOR'S NOTE : The term *episteme* corresponds better to the bundle of meanings included in our words " knowledge " and " understanding ". For the astonishment occasioned by the novel term *philosophia*, see Cicero, *Tusculan Disputations*, V, 3.

C

Science is one of the most sublime pursuits and achievements of mankind : more sublime than the university itself, conceived as an educational institution. For science is creation, and teaching aims only at conveying what has been created, to digest. it and to induce learners to digest it. Science is carried on upon so high a plane that it is necessarily an extremely delicate process. Whether we like it or not, science excludes the ordinary man. It involves a calling most infrequent, and remote from the ordinary run of the human species. The scientist is the monk of modern times.

To pretend that the normal student is a scientist, is at once a ridiculous pretension, which could scarcely have been contracted (pretensions are contracted, like colds and other inflammations) but for that vice of utopianism, the bane of the generation just preceding ours. But furthermore it is not desirable, even under ideal circumstances, that the ordinary man should be a scientist. If science is one of the highest of human pursuits, it is not the only one. There are others of equal dignity, and there is no reason to sacrifice these, dedicating all humanity to science. The sublimity, moreover, belongs to science itself and not to the man of science. His career is a mode of existence quite as limited and narrow as another ; in fact more so than some you could imagine. Here I cannot embark on an analysis of what it means to be a scientist. Nor do I wish to. It would be out of place, and besides, some of what I should say might seem unpleasant. Returning then to the essential matter, let me observe that up to our time at least, the *real* scientist, considered as a person, has been with notorious frequency a visionary and a freak, when he has not been absolutely demented. The real marvel, the precious thing, is what this very limited person succeeds in isolating : the pearl, not the oyster that secreted it. It is futile to idealize the scientist and hold him up as the model for all men to imitate, without taking into account the complex circumstances—miraculous, some of them, and some of them quite unfathomable—which are wont to enter into the making of the scientist.[1]

The teaching of the professions and the search for truth *must* be separated. They must be clearly distinguished one from the other, both in the minds of the professors and in the minds of

[1] AUTHOR'S NOTE : It is notorious for example how readily scientists have always acquiesced in tyrannical governments. This is no cause for disappointment, nor can it be considered a liability to society. The cause of it lies in the very nature of the scientist, and is perfectly respectable.

the students. For their present confusion is an impediment to science. Granted, the apprenticeship to some professions in-cludes as a very important element the mastery of the systematized content of numerous sciences ; but this content is the end result of investigation, and not the investigation itself. As a general principle, the normal student is not an apprentice to science. The physician is learning to effect cures, and as a physician he need not go beyond that. For his purpose, he needs to know the system of physiology current in his day, but he need not be, and in fact cannot be expected to be, a trained physiologist. Why do we persist in expecting the impossible ? I cannot understand. I am only disgusted by this itching to delude oneself—" you *have* to have your illusions "—this everlasting delusion of grandeur, this die-hard utopianism of persuading ourselves that we are achieving what we are not. Utopianism results in a pedagogy of self-abuse.

It is the virtue of the child to think in terms of wishes, it is the child's rôle to make believe. But the virtue of the grown man is to will, and his rôle is to do and achieve. Now we can achieve things only by concentrating our energy : by limiting ourselves. And in this limiting of ourselves lies the truth and the authenticity of our life. Indeed, all life is destiny : if our existence were unlimited in duration and in the forms it could assume, there would be no " destiny ".[1] The authentic life, young people, consists in cheerfully accepting an inexorable destiny—a limitation we cannot alter. It is this state of mind which the mystics, following a profound intuition, used to call " the state of grace ". He who has once honestly accepted his destiny, his own limitations, is imperturable. " *Impavidum ferient ruinae.*"

If a man has the calling to be a physician and nothing more, let him not dabble in science. He will but turn science into mediocrity. It is enough, in fact it is everything, that he is a good physician. The same holds in my opinion for the man who is to be a good professor of history in a secondary school. Is it not a mistake to confuse him in college by making him think he is going to be a historian ? What do you gain ? You force him to consume his time in a fragmentary study of tech-

---

[1] EDITOR'S NOTE : Ortega's term " destino " presents much the same difficulty as Aristotle's two terms δύναμις and ἐνέργεια, for which English translators have found no satisfying translation. The organism is conceived as being endowed with a specific *potentiality*, whose *realization* constitutes the organism's proper life. The term " destiny ", as well as another, will take on the intended meaning as the essay proceeds.

niques necessary to the research of the historian, but irrelevant to the teaching of history. You excuse him from that other task of achieving a clear, organized, comprehensible idea of the general body of human history, which it is his mission to teach.[1]

The trend towards a university dominated by " inquiry " has been disastrous. It has led to the elimination of the prime concern : culture. It has deflected attention from the problem of how best to train future professionals for their professions.

The medical schools aspire to teach physiology and chemistry complete to the nth degree ; but perhaps in no medical school the world over is there anyone seriously occupied with thinking out what it really means to be a good physician, what the ideal type should be for our times. The profession, which after culture is the most urgent concern, is entrusted largely to the kindness of Providence. But the harm of our confused procedure has worked both ways. Science too has suffered by our wishful attempt to bring it into line alongside the professions.

Pedantry and the lack of reflection have been large causes in bringing on the " scientism " which afflicted the university. In Spain, both these deplorable forces are coming to be a serious nuisance. Any nincompoop who has been six months in a school or a laboratory in Germany or North America, any parrot who has made a third-rate scientific discovery, comes back a *nouveau riche* of science. Without having reflected a quarter of an hour on the mission of the university, he propounds the most pedantic and ridiculous reforms. Moreover he is incapable of teaching his own courses, for he has no grasp of the discipline as a whole.

We must therefore shake science off the tree of the professions, and retain only the portion of science which is strictly necessary, in order to attend to the professions themselves, whose teaching, to-day, runs quite wild. At this step everything is still to be begun.[2]

Logical organization and ingenious teaching will make it possible to teach the professions much more efficiently and with greater breadth, with less time and effort than at present.

But now let us proceed to that other distinction, between science and culture.

[1] AUTHOR'S NOTE : It is obvious that he must learn what composes the techniques by which history is obtained. But this does not mean that he must become an adept, himself, in these techniques.

[2] AUTHOR'S NOTE : The basic idea, the prototype of each profession—what it means to be a doctor, judge, lawyer, professor, etc.—is not at present delineated in the popular mind, nor does anyone devote himself to studying and formulating such an idea.

CHAPTER V

CULTURE AND SCIENCE

If we review in substance the distinction between profession and science, we find ourselves in possession of a few clear ideas. For example, medicine is not a science but a profession, a matter of practice. Hence it represents a point of view distinct from that of science. It proposes as its object to restore and maintain health in the human species. To this end, it appropriates what it finds useful : it goes to science and takes whatever results of research it considers efficacious ; but it leaves all the rest. It leaves particularly what is most characteristic of science : the cultivation of the problematic and doubtful. This would suffice to differentiate radically between medicine and science. Science consists in an urge to solve problems ; the more it is engaged in this occupation, the more purely it accomplishes its mission. But medicine exists for the purpose of applying solutions. If they happen to be scientific, so much the better. But they are not necessarily so. They may have grown out of some millennial experience which science has not yet explained or even confirmed.

In the last fifty years, medicine has allowed itself to be swept off its feet by science ; it has neglected its own mission and failed to assert properly its own professional point of view.[1] Medicine has committed the besetting sin of that whole period : namely, to look askance at destiny and strain to be something else—in this case, pure science.

Let us make no mistake about it. Science, upon entering into a profession, must be detached from its place in pure science, to be organized upon a new centre and a new principle, as professional technics. And if this is true, it must certainly have an effect on the teaching of the professions.

Something similar is to be said of the relations between culture and science. The difference between them seems to me clear enough. Yet I should like not only to leave the con-

[1] AUTHOR'S NOTE : On the other hand, when medicine has devoted itself to its proper function of curing, its work has proved most fruitful for science. Contemporary physiology was launched on its career, early in the last century, not by the scientists but by the physicians, who turned aside from the scholasticism that had reigned over eighteenth century biology (taxonomy, anatomism, etc.) to meet their urgent mission with pragmatic theories. See Emanuel Radl, *Geschichte der biologischen Theorien*, vol. II (1909), a book which seems the more admirable with the passing of time.

C*

cept of culture very definite in the mind of the reader but also
to show what basis it has. First, the reader must go to the
trouble of scrutinizing and reflecting upon the following résumé
—which will not be easy : culture is the system of vital ideas which
each age possesses ; better yet, it is the system of ideas *by* which
the age lives. There is no denying the fact that man invariably
lives according to some definite ideas which constitute the very
foundation of his way of life. These ideas which I have called
" vital ", meaning ideas by which an age conducts its life, are no
more nor less than the repertory of our *active* convictions as to the
nature of our world and our fellow creatures, convictions as to the
hierarchy of the values of things—which are more to be esteemed,
and which less.[1]

It is not in our hands whether to possess such a repertory of
convictions or not. It is a matter of inescapable necessity, an
ingredient essential to every human life, of whatever sort it may
be. The reality we are wont to refer to as " human life ", your
life and the next fellow's, is something quite remote from biology,
the science of organisms. Biology, like any other science, is
no more than one occupation to which some men devote their
" life ". The basic and truest meaning of the word *life* is not
biological but biographical : and that is the meaning it has always
had in the language of the people. It means the totality of what
we do and what we are—that formidable business, which every
man must exercise on his own, of maintaining a place in the
scheme of things and steering a course among the beings of the
world. " To live is, in fact, to have dealings with the world :
to address oneself to it, exert oneself in it, and occupy oneself
with it." [2] If these actions and occupations which compose our
living were produced in us mechanically, the result would not be
human life. The automaton does not *live*. The whole difficulty
of the matter is that life is not given us ready made. Like it or
not, we must go along from instant to instant, deciding for ourselves. At each moment it is necessary to make up our minds
what we are going to do next : the life of man is an ever-recurrent
problem. In order to decide at one instant what he is going
to do or to be at the next, man is compelled to form a plan of
some sort, however simple or puerile it may be. It is not that

[1] EDITOR'S NOTE : Cf. Ortega's *The Modern Theme*, p. 76 : " Culture is merely
a special direction which we give to the cultivation of our animal potencies."

[2] AUTHOR'S NOTE : I have borrowed this formula from my essay *El Estado, la
juventud y el carnaval*, published in *La Nación*, of Buenos Aires, December 1924, and
reprinted in *El Espectador* (VII).

he *ought* to make a plan. There is simply no possible life, sublime or mean, wise or stupid, which is not essentially characterized by its proceeding with reference to some plan.[1] Even to abandon our life to chance, in a moment of despair, is to make a plan. Every human being, perforce, picks his way through life. Or what comes to the same, as he decides upon each act he performs, he does so *because* that act " seems best ", given the circumstances. This is tantamount to saying that every life is obliged, willy-nilly, to justify itself in its own eyes. Self-justification is a constituent part of our life. We refer to one and the same fact, whether we say that " to live is to conduct oneself according to a plan ", or that " life is a continuous justification to oneself ". But this plan or justification implies that we have acquired some " idea " of the world and the things in it, and also of our potential acts which have bearing upon it. In short, man cannot live without reacting to his environment with some rudimentary concept of it. He is forced to make an intellectual interpretation of the world about him, and of his conduct in it. This interpretation is the repertory of ideas or convictions to which I have referred, and which, as it is now perfectly evident, cannot be lacking in any human life whatsoever.[2]

The vast majority of these convictions or ideas are not fabricated by the individual, Crusoe-wise, but simply received by him from his historical environment—his times. Naturally, any age presents very disparate systems of convictions. Some are a drossy residue of other times. But there is always a system of live ideas which represents the superior level of the age, a system which is essentially characteristic of its times ; and this system is the culture of the age. He who lives at a lower level, on archaic ideas, condemns himself to a lower life, more difficult, toilsome, unrefined. This is the plight of backward peoples— or individuals. They ride through life in an ox-cart while others speed by them in automobiles. Their concept of the world wants truth, it wants richness, and it wants acumen. The man who lives

[1] AUTHOR'S NOTE : The sublimity or meanness of a life, its wisdom or stupidity is, precisely, its plan. Obviously our plan does not remain the same for life ; it may vary continually. The essential fact is that life and plan are inseparable.

[2] AUTHOR'S NOTE : It is easy to see that when an element of our life so fundamental as this self-justification functions irregularly, the ailment which ensues is grave. Such is the case with the curious type of man I have studied in *The Revolt of the Masses*. But the first edition of that book is incomplete. A prolonged illness prevented me from finishing it. In the later editions [not yet appeared, Oct. 1944–ED.] I am adding the third part of the study, analysing more in detail this formidable problem of " justification ", and thus adding the finishing touch to that book's investigation into this very prevalent phenomenon.

on a plane beneath the enlightened level of his time is condemned, relatively, to the life of an infra-man.

In our age, the content of culture comes largely from science. But our discussion suffices to indicate that culture is not science. The content of culture, though it is being made in the field of science more than elsewhere, is not scientific fact but rather a vital faith, a conviction characteristic of our times. Five hundred years ago, faith was reposed in ecclesiastical councils, and the content of culture emanated in large part from them.

Culture does with science, therefore, the same thing the profession does. It borrows from science what is vitally necessary for the interpretation of our existence. There are entire portions of science which are not culture, but pure scientific technique. And vice versa, culture requires that we possess a complete concept of the world and of man ; it is not for culture to stop, with science, at the point where the methods of absolute theoretic rigour happen to end. Life cannot wait until the sciences may have explained the universe scientifically. We cannot put off living until we are ready. The most salient characteristic of life is its coerciveness : it is always urgent, " here and now," without any possible postponement. Life is fired at us point-blank. And culture, which is but its interpretation, cannot wait any more than can life itself.

This sharpens the distinction between culture and the sciences. Science is not something by which we live. If the physicist had to live by the ideas of his science, you may rest assured that he would not be so finicky as to wait for some other investigator to complete his research a century or so later. He would renounce the hope of a complete scientific solution, and fill in, with approximate or probable anticipations, what the rigorous corpus of physical doctrine lacks at present, and in part, always will lack.

The internal conduct of science is not a *vital* concern ; that of culture is. Science is indifferent to the exigencies of our life, and follows its own necessities. Accordingly, science grows constantly more diversified and specialized without limit, and is never completed. But culture is subservient to our life here and now, and is required to be, at every instant, a complete, unified, coherent system—the plan of life, the path leading through the forest of existence.

That metaphor of ideas as paths or roads (*methodoi*) is as old as culture itself. Its origin is evident. When we find ourselves in a perplexing, confused situation, it is as though we stood before a dense forest, through whose tangles we cannot advance without being lost. Someone explains the situation, with a happy idea, and we experience a sudden illumination —the "light" of understanding. The thicket immediately appears ordered, and the lines of its structure seem like paths opening through it. Hence the term *method* is regularly associated with that of enlightenment, illumination, *Aufklärung*. What we call to-day "a cultured man" was called more than a century ago "an enlightened man", i.e. a man who sees the paths of life in a clear light.

Let us cast away once for all those vague notions of enlightenment and culture, which make them appear as some sort of ornamental accessory for the life of leisure. There could not be a falser misrepresentation. Culture is an indispensable element of life, a dimension of our existence, as much a part of man as his hands. True, there is such a thing as man without hands ; but that is no longer simply man : it is man crippled. The same is to be said of life without culture, only in a much more fundamental sense. It is a life crippled, wrecked, false. The man who fails to live at the height of his time is living beneath what would constitute his right life. Or in other words, he is swindling himself out of his own life.

We are passing at present, despite certain appearances and presumptions, through an age of terrific *un-culture*. Never perhaps has the ordinary man been so far below his times and what they demand of him. Never has the civilized world so abounded in falsified, cheated lives. Almost nobody is poised squarely upon his proper and authentic place in life. Man is habituated to living on subterfuges with which he deceives himself, conjuring up around him a very simple and arbitrary world, in spite of the admonitions of an active conscience which forces him to observe that his real world, the world that corresponds to the whole of actuality, is one of enormous complexity and grim urgency. But he is afraid—our ordinary man is timorous at heart, with all his brave gesticulations—he is afraid to admit this real world, which would make great demands on him. He prefers to falsify his life, and keep it sealed up in the cocoon of his fictitious, oversimplified concept of the world.[1]

[1] AUTHOR'S NOTE : On this subject in general see *The Revolt of the Masses* in its next edition [not yet published, Oct. 1944–ED.], where I deal more in detail with the specific ways in which the people of to-day are falsifying their lives : for example, the naïve belief that " you have to be arbitrary ", from which has issued in politics the lie of Fascism, and in letters and philosophy, the young Spanish " intellectual " of recent years.

Hence the historic importance of restoring to the university its cardinal function of " enlightenment ", the task of imparting the full culture of the time and revealing to mankind, with clarity and truthfulness, that gigantic world of to-day in which the life of the individual must be articulated, if it is to be authentic.

Personally, I should make a Faculty of Culture the nucleus of the university and of the whole higher learning.[1] I have already sketched the outline of its disciplines. Each of these, it will be remembered, bears two names : for example " The physical scheme of the world (Physics) ". This dual designation is intended to suggest the difference between a cultural discipline, vitally related to life, and the corresponding science by which it is nurtured. The " Faculty " of Culture would not expound physics as the science is presented to a student intending to devote his life to physico-mathematical research. The physics in culture is the rigorously derived synthesis of ideas about the nature and functioning of the physical cosmos, as these ideas have emerged from the physical research so far completed. In addition, this discipline will analyse the means of acquiring knowledge, by which the physicist has achieved his marvellous construction ; it will therefore be necessary to expound the principles of physics, and to trace, briefly but scrupulously, the course of their historical evolution. This last element of the course will enable the student to visualize what the " world " was, in which man lived a generation or a century or a thousand years ago ; and by contrast, he will be able to realize and appreciate the peculiarities of our " world " of to-day.

This is the time to answer an objection which arose at the beginning of my essay, and was postponed. How—it is asked —can the present-day concept of matter be made intelligible to anyone who is not versed in higher mathematics ? Every day, mathematical method makes some new advance at the very base of physical science.

[1] EDITOR'S NOTE : The form of this proposal has been objected to by readers of the manuscript on the ground that it gives too much responsibility and too much power to one group. The American college or university might better seek to solve the administrative problem through a committee representative of the whole faculty, serving as the spearhead for the reform yet democratically stimulating and co-ordinating the initiative arising from all parts of the institution. Another committee of the whole faculty might be made responsible for improving the conditions for research ; and each professional department might appoint a committee of appropriate academic and community representatives to examine how the occupational training can be oriented towards a richer service to society. This adaptation of Ortega's basic idea has been elaborated in the editor's forthcoming book on cultural education and intercultural synthesis, tentatively scheduled to be published in 1945 by Harper and Brothers.

I should like the reader to consider the tragedy without escape which would confront humanity if the view implied here were correct. Either everyone would be obliged to be a thorough physicist, devoting himself, dedicating his life,[1] to research in order not to live inept and devoid of insight into the world we live in ; or else most of us must resign ourselves to an existence which, in one of its dimensions, is doomed to stupidity. The physicist would be for the man in the street like some being endowed with a magical, hieratic knowledge. Both of these solutions would be—among other things—ridiculous.

But fortunately there is no such dilemma. In the first place, the doctrine I am defending calls for a thorough rationalizing of the methods of instruction, from the primary grades to the university. Precisely by recognizing science to be a thing apart, we pave the way to the segregating of its cultural elements so that these may be made assimilable. The " principle of economy in education " is not satisfied by extruding disciplines the student cannot learn ; it requires economy in the teaching of what remains to be taught. Economy in these two respects would add a new margin to the learning capacity of the student, so that he could actually learn more than at present.[2] I believe, then, that in time to come no student will arrive at the university without being already acquainted with the mathematics of physics, sufficiently at least to be capable of understanding its formulas.

Mathematicians exaggerate a bit the difficulties of their subject. It is an extensive one but, after all, it is always expressible in definite terms to anyone who " knows beans ". If it appears so incomprehensible to-day, it is because the necessary energy has not been applied to the simplifying of its teaching, This affords me an opportunity to proclaim for the first time, and with due solemnity, that if we fail to cultivate this sort of intellectual effort—effort addressed not to descriptive analysis, after the usual manner of research, but to the task of simplifying and synthesizing the quintessence of science, without sacrifice of its quality or substantialness—then the future of science itself will be disastrous.

It is imperative that the present dispersion and complication of scientific labours be counterbalanced by the complementary

[1] AUTHOR'S NOTE : It is to be noted that any dedicating of oneself, if it is real, means the dedication of one's life and nothing less.

[2] AUTHOR'S NOTE : Precisely because of the efficiency in the teaching, a greater power to learn is called into action.

kind of scientific activity, striving towards the concentration and consolidation of knowledge. We need to develop a special type of talent, for the specific function of synthesizing. The destiny of science is at stake.

But, in the second place, I deny roundly that in order to grasp the fundamental ideas—the principles, the methods of procedure, the end results—of any science which has fundamental ideas to offer, the student must necessarily have had formal training and become familiar with its techniques. The truth is quite otherwise. When a science, in its internal development, proceeds towards ideas which require technical familiarity in order to be understood, then its ideas are losing their fundamental character to become instruments subordinate to the science, rather than its substance proper.[1] The mastery of higher mathematics is essential for *making* the science but not for understanding its import for human life.

It happens, at once luckily and unluckily, that the nation which stands gloriously and indisputably in the van of science is Germany. The German, in addition to his prodigious talent and inclination for science, has a congenital weakness which it would be extremely hard to extirpate : he is *a nativitate* pedantic and impervious of mind. This fact has brought it about that not a few sides of our present-day science are not really science, but only pedantic detail, all too easily and credulously gathered together. One of the tasks Europe needs to perform with dispatch is to rid contemporary science of its purely German excrescences, its rituals and mere whims, in order to save its essential parts uncontaminated.[2]

Europe cannot be saved without a return to intellectual discipline, and this discipline needs to be more rigorous than those which have been used or abused in other times. No one must be allowed to escape. Not even the man of science. To-day this personage conserves not a little of feudal violence, egotism and arrogance, vanity and pontification.

There is need to humanize the scientist, who rebelled, about the middle of the last century, and to his shame let himself be contaminated by the gospel of insubordination which has been

[1] AUTHOR'S NOTE : In the last analysis, mathematics is wholly instrumental in character, not fundamental or substantial in itself—just as is that branch of science which studies the microscope.

[2] AUTHOR'S NOTE : Do not forget, in seeking to grasp the implications of this opinion, that the writer of it owes to Germany four-fifths of his intellectual possessions. I am more conscious to-day than ever before of the indisputable, towering pre-eminence of German science. The question alluded to has nothing to do with this.

since then the great vulgarity and the great falsity of the age.[1] The man of science can no longer afford to be what he now is with lamentable frequency—a barbarian knowing much of one thing. Fortunately the principal figures in the present generation of scientists have felt impelled by the internal necessities of their sciences to balance their specialization with a symmetrical culture. The rest will follow in their steps as sheep follow the leading ram.

From all quarters the need presses upon us for a new integration of knowledge, which to-day lies in pieces scattered over the world. But the labour of this undertaking is enormous ; it is not to be thought of while there exists no methodology of higher education even comparable to what we have for the preceding levels of education. At present we lack completely a pedagogy of the university—though this statement seems untrue at first.

It has come to be an imminent problem, one which mankind can no longer evade, to invent a technique adequate to cope with the accumulation of knowledge now in our possession. Unless some practicable way is found to master this exuberant growth, man will eventually become its victim. On top of the primitive forest of life we would only add the forest of science, whose intention was to simplify the first. If science has brought order into life we shall now have to put science in order, organize it—seeing that it is impossible to regiment science—for the sake of its healthy perpetuation. To this end we must vitalize science : that is, we must provide it with a form compatible with the human life by which and for which it was made in the first place. Otherwise—for there is no use in entrenching ourselves behind a vague optimism—otherwise science will cease to function ; mankind will lose interest in it.

And so you see that by thinking over what is the mission of the university, by seeking to discover the consequent character of its cultural disciplines (viz. systematic and synthetic), we come out upon a vast horizon that spreads quite beyond the field of pedagogy, and engages us to see in the institution of higher learning an agent for the salvation of science itself.

[1] AUTHOR'S NOTE : The great task of the present age, in the field of morality, is to convince common men (uncommon men never fell into the snare) of the inane foolishness which envelops this urge to revolt, and make them see the cheap facility, the meanness of it ; even though we may freely admit that most of the things revolted against deserve to be buried away. The only true revolt is creation—the revolt against nothingness. Lucifer is the patron saint of mere negativistic revolt.

The need to create sound syntheses and systematizations of knowledge, to be taught in the " Faculty of Culture ", will call out a kind of scientific genius which hitherto has existed only as an aberration : the genius for integration. Of necessity this means specialization, as all creative effort inevitably does ; but this time, the man will be specializing in the construction of a whole. The momentum which impels investigation to dissociate indefinitely into particular problems, the pulverization of research, makes necessary a compensative control—as in any healthy organism—which is to be furnished by a force pulling in the opposite direction, constraining centrifugal science in a wholesome organization.

Men endowed with this genius come nearer being good professors than those who are submerged in their research. One of the evils attending the confusion of the university with science has been the awarding of professorships, in keeping with the mania of the times, to research workers who are nearly always very poor professors, and regard their teaching as time stolen away from their work in the laboratory or the archives. This was brought home to me by experience during my years of study in Germany. I have lived close to a good number of the foremost scientists of our time, yet I have not found among them a single good teacher [1]—so let no one come and tell me that the German university, as an institution, is a model !

[1] AUTHOR'S NOTE : Which does not mean that none exist ; but it does indicate that the combination does not occur with any dependable frequency.

CHAPTER VI

WHAT THE UNIVERSITY MUST BE " IN ADDITION "

The " principle of economy ", which amounts to the determination to see things as they are and not as a Utopian illusion,
has led us to define the primary mission of the university in
this wise :

1. The university, in the strict sense, is to mean that institution
which teaches the ordinary student to be a cultured person and
a good member of a profession.

2. The university will not tolerate in its programme any
false pretence : it will profess to require of the student only
what actually can be required of him.

3. It will consequently avoid causing the ordinary student to
waste part of his time in pretending that he is going to be a
scientist. To this end, scientific investigation proper is to be
eliminated from the core or minimum of the university.

4. The cultural disciplines and the professional studies will
be offered in a rationalized form based on the best pedagogy—
systematic, synthetic, and complete—and not in the form which
science would prefer, if it were left to itself : special problems,
" samples " of science, and experimentation.

5. The selection of professors will depend not on their rank
as investigators but on their talent for synthesis and their gift for
teaching.

6. When the student's apprenticeship has been reduced to the
minimum, both quantitatively and qualitatively, the university
will be inflexible in its requirements from him.

This ascetic frugality of pretensions, this severe loyalty in
recognizing the limits of the attainable, will, in my belief, procure
what is the university's most fundamental need : the need that
its institutional life correspond squarely to its proper functions
and true limits, in order that its life may be genuine and sincere
in its inmost dealings. I have already proposed that the new life
should take as its point of departure this simple recognition of the
destiny of the individual or of the institution. All else that we
may subsequently wish to make of ourselves, or of private institutions or the state, will take root and come to fruition only if we
have planted its seed in the rich soil of a nature resigned to be,

first of all, the essential minimum which corresponds to its destiny. Europe is sick because its people profess to stand upon a precarious tenth rung in life, without having taken the trouble first to secure a footing on the elemental one, two, three. Destiny is the only bedrock on which human life and all its aspirations can stand. Life on any other basis is false. It has no authentic personality, it is something up in the air. It lacks a local habitation and a name.

Now we can open our minds without fear or reservation, to consider all that the university should be " in addition."

Indeed, the university, as we have defined it for the nonce, cannot be that alone. And now is the proper time for us to recognize, in all its breadth and depth, the rôle science must play in the physiology of the university, or rather let us say its psychology, for the university is better to be compared with a spirit than a body.

In the first place, we have seen that culture and profession are not science, but are largely nourished by science. Without science, the destiny of the European man would be an impossibility. The European man represents, in the panorama of history, the being resolved to live according to his intellect ; and science is but intellect " in form ". Is it perchance a mere accident that only the European has possessed universities, among so many peoples ? The university *is* the intellect, it *is* science, erected into an institution. And this institutionalizing of intellect is the originality of the European compared with other races, other lands, and other ages. It signifies the peculiar resolution adopted by the European man, to live according to the dictates of his intelligence. Others have chosen to live according to other faculties. Remember the marvellous laconisms in which Hegel sums up universal history, like an alchemist reducing tons of carbon to a few diamonds : Persia, land of Light ! (referring to mystical religion) ; Greece, land of Grace ! India, land of Dream ! Rome, land of Empire ! [1]

Europe is the intelligence. A wonderful power : it is the only power which perceives its own limitations—and thereby it proves how intelligent it is ! This power which is its own restraint finds in science the scope for its full grandeur.

If culture and the professions were to be isolated in the

---

[1] AUTHOR'S NOTE : Hegel, *Lectures on the Philosophy of History* (translated from the third German edition by J. Sibree, London, 1861 : see pp. xxix ff.).

university and to have no contact with the incessant ferment of science, of investigation of all sorts, it would not be long before they would be overtaken by the creeping paralysis of scholasticism. Around the central part of the university, the sciences must pitch their camps—their laboratories and seminars and discussion centres. The sciences are the soil out of which the higher learning grows and from which it draws its sustenance. Accordingly its roots must reach out to the laboratories of every sort and tap them for the nourishment they can provide. All normal university students will come and go between the university and these outlying camps of the sciences, where they will find courses conceived from an exclusively scientific point of view, on all things human and divine. Of the professors, those who are more amply gifted will be investigators as well, and the others, who are purely teachers, will work none the less in closest contact with science, under its criticism and the influence of its ferment and stimulation. What is inadmissible is the confusion of the central portion of the university with the zone of research surrounding its borders. The university and the laboratory are distinct, correlative organs in a complete physiology. The essential difference between them is that only the university proper is to be characterized as an institution. Science is an activity too sublime and subtle to be organized in an institution. Science is neither to be coerced nor regimented. Hence it is harmful, both for the higher learning and for investigation, to attempt to fuse them into one instead of letting them work hand in hand in an exchange of influence as free and spontaneous as it is intense.

Thus the university is distinct from science yet inseparable from it. I should say myself, " The university *is* science *in addition*."

Not, however, the simple " addition " of an increment set down in merely external proximity to the institution. Quite the contrary. And now we may make the point without fear of misunderstanding. The university must *be* science before it can be a university. An atmosphere charged with enthusiasm, the exertion of science, is the presupposition at the base of the university's existence. Precisely because the institution cannot be composed of science—the unrestricted creation of exact knowledge—it requires the spirit of science to animate its institutional life. Unless this spirit is presupposed, all that has been said in the present essay has no sense. Science is the dignity of the university—and more, for life is possible without dignity : it is the soul of the institution, the principle which gives it the breath of life and saves it from being an automaton. That is the sense in which the university " is science, in addition."

But it is still more.[1] Not only does it need perpetual contact with science, on pain of atrophy ; it needs contact, likewise, with the public life, with historical reality, with the present, which is essentially a whole to be dealt with only in its totality, not after amputations *ad usum Delphini*. The university must be open to the whole reality of its time. It must be in the midst of real life, and saturated with it.

And all this not only because it suits the purpose of the university to live in the quickening atmosphere of historical reality. Conversely as well, the life of the people needs acutely to have the university participate, *as* the university, in its affairs.

On this point there is much I should like to say. But to be brief, let me simply allude to the fact that in the collective life of society to-day there is no other " spiritual power " than the press. The corporate life, which is the real life of history,[2] needs always to be directed, whether we like the idea or not. Of itself it has no form, no eyes to see with, no guiding sense of direction. Now then, in our times, the ancient " spiritual powers " have disappeared : the Church because it has abandoned the present (whereas the life of the people is ever a decidedly current affair) ; and the state because with the triumph of democracy it has given up governing the life of the people, to be governed instead by their opinion. In this situation, the public life has devolved into the hands of the only spiritual force which necessarily concerns itself with current affairs—the press.

I should not wish to throw too many stones at the journalists ; among other motives, there is the consideration that I may be nothing more than a journalist myself. But it is futile to shut our eyes to the obvious fact that spiritual realities differ in worth. They compose a hierarchy of values, and in this hierarchy,

[1] AUTHOR'S NOTE : I have deliberately refrained in this essay from even naming the topic of moral education in the university, in order to devote undivided attention to the problem of intellectual content.

[2] EDITOR'S NOTE : Sr. Ortega has discussed this concept—that " cultures are organisms and are the true subjects for history "—in *Las Atlántidas* (Madrid, 1924), especially p. xxiv, and in the foreword which he wrote for the Spanish edition of Spengler's *Decline of the West*. Sr. Ortega mentions that he had arrived at the concept independently of Spengler. For a discussion of the difficulties that have since discredited the conception of a society as an organism, see Melvin Rader, *No Compromise* (Macmillan, 1939), pp. 239 ff. and 306 ff. See also the essays of Ortega assembled by Mrs. Helene Weyl in *Towards a Philosophy of History*, New York : W. W. Norton, 1941.

journalism occupies an inferior place. It has come to pass that to-day no pressure and no authority make themselves felt in the public consciousness, save on the very low spiritual plane adopted by the emanations of the press. So low a plane it is that not infrequently the press falls quite short of being a spiritual power, and is rather the opposite force. By the default of other powers, the responsibility for nourishing and guiding the public soul has fallen to the journalist, who not only is one of the least cultured types in contemporary society but who moreover—for reasons I hope may prove to have been merely transitory—admits into his profession the frustrated pseudo-intellectuals, full of resentment and hatred towards what is truly spiritual. Furthermore the journalist's profession leads him to understand by the reality of the times that which creates a passing sensation, regardless of what it is, without any heed for perspective or architecture. Real life is, certainly, purely of the present ; but the journalist deforms this truism when he reduces the present to the momentary, and the momentary to the sensational. The result is that, in the public consciousness to-day, the image of the world appears exactly upside down. The space devoted to people and affairs in the press is inversely proportional to their substantial and enduring importance ; what stands out in the columns of the newspapers and magazines is what will be a " success " and bring notoriety. Were the periodicals to be freed from motives that are often unspeakable ; were the dailies kept chastely aloof from any influence of money in their opinions—the press would still, of itself, forsake its proper mission and paint the world inside out. Not a little of the grotesque and general upset of our age—(for Europe has been going along for some time now with her head on the ground and her plebeian feet waving in the air)—is the result of this unchallenged sway of the press as sole " spiritual power ".

It is a question of life and death for Europe to put this ridiculous situation to rights. And if this is to be done the university must intervene, *as* the university, in current affairs, treating the great themes of the day from its own point of view : cultural, professional, and scientific.[1] Thus it will not be an institution exclusively for students, a retreat *ad usum Delphini*. In the thick of life's urgencies and its passions, the university must assert

---

[1] AUTHOR'S NOTE : It is inconceivable, for example, that in the face of a problem such as that of foreign exchange, which now preoccupies Spain, the university should not be offering the serious public a course on this difficult economic question.

itself as a major "spiritual power", higher than the press, standing for serenity in the midst of frenzy, for seriousness and the grasp of intellect in the face of frivolity and unashamed stupidity.

Then the university, once again, will come to be what it was in its grand hour : an uplifting principle in the history of the western world.

INDEX

Towards a Philosophy of History, 76 n. *See also* "History as a System"

Toynbee, Arnold, 16, 18–20

UNIVERSITY, function in present society, 39–43 ; guilt of the 19th-century university, 45 ; medieval, 21, 43, 56 ; Ortega's proposal "dated", 20 ; proper functions, 73–6 ; responsibility for a synthesis and dissemination of it, 17, 44, 58 ; suggested "Faculty of Culture", 68–70 (adapted to U.S.) 68 n. ; Synthesis Seminar, 24. *See also* Professions, School and society,

Sciences, Students, Synthesis of culture, need of

Valuation, 11, 12 ; need for rational valuation, 15 ; postulates may conflict interculturally, 22 ; universal values, 20 ; value judgments inevitable, 20, 64–5. *See also* Dualism, Human nature, Synthesis of culture, "Vital ideas"

"Vital ideas," 44, 58, 64–6, 69–70. *See also* General education, Synthesis of culture

Weyl, Helene, 4, 27 n., 76 n.

Whitehead, Alfred North, 9, 13, 14, 16 n.

The International Library of
SOCIOLOGY AND SOCIAL RECONSTRUCTION
Editor: KARL MANNHEIM

PLAN OF THE LIBRARY
Sections

KEGAN PAUL, TRENCH, TRUBNER & CO. LTD.
68-74 Carter Lane, London, E.C.4

SOCIOLOGY OF EDUCATION

Mission of the University
by ORTEGA Y GASSET. Translated and introduced by HOWARD LEE
NOSTRAND
About 8s. 6d.

Total Education: A Plea for Synthesis
by M. L. JACKS, Director, Department of Education, Oxford University
10s. 6d.

Education in Transition
A Sociological Analysis of the Impact of the War on English Education
by H. C. DENT
Fourth Impression. 12s. 6d.

The Reform of Secondary Education
by H. C. DENT
About 15s.

The Education of the Countryman
by H. M. BURTON
Second Impression. 15s.

Education for Adults: A Study in Transition
by T. MACKAY MURE
About 10s. 6d.

Adult Education in a Progressive Democracy
Historical Studies and a Programme for the Future by H. E. POOLE,
Organising Secretary of the W.E.A., Norfolk; PAUL H. SHEATS,
Professor of Education, Pres. of the Dept. of Adult Education of the
Nat. Educ. Assoc., U.S.A.; DAVID CUSHMAN COYLE, U.S.A., Assistant
Director of Town Hall, New York; E. BORINSKI, Dr. Phil. *About 21s.*

Who Shall Be Educated? The Challenge of Unequal Opportunities
by W. LLOYD WARNER, Prof. of Anthropology and Sociology, Member
of Comm. on Human Development, Univ. of Chicago; ROBERT J.
HAVIGHURST, Prof. of Education, Member of Comm. on Human
Development, Univ. of Chicago; MARTIN B. LOEB, Inst. of Child
Welfare, Univ. of California, at Berkeley *In preparation. About 15s. net*

Natural Science and Education: A Sociological Study
by J. A. LAUWERYS, Reader in Education in the Univ. of London
About 15s.

The Social Psychology of Education: A Sociological Study

by C. M. FLEMING, Ed.B., Ph.D., University of London Institute of Education   *Third Impression. 7s. 6d.*

German Youth: Bond or Free?

by HOWARD BECKER, Professor of Sociology, University of Wisconsin
In preparation. Illustrated. About 15s.

The Museum: Its History and Its Tasks in Education

by ALMA S. WITTLIN, Dr. Phil.   *In preparation. Illustrated. About 21s.*

SOCIOLOGY OF RELIGION

The Sociology of Religion

by JOACHIM WACH   *About 10s. 6d.*

Religion and the Economic Order

by FRANK KNIGHT, Prof. of Social Sciences, University of Chicago, and THORNTON W. MERRIAM, Director of U.S.O. Training Nat. Council of the Y.M.C.A.   *In preparation. About 21s.*

SOCIOLOGY OF ART

Sociology of the Renaissance

by ALFRED VON MARTIN, translated by W. L. LUETKENS
Second Impression. 8s. 6d.

SOCIOLOGY OF LANGUAGE AND LITERATURE

The Sociology of Literary Taste

by LEVIN L. SCHÜCKING, Dr. Phil.   *Second Impression. 7s. 6d.*

Authors and the Public in Eighteenth-Century England
by ALEXANDRE BELJAME. Edited with an Introduction by Prof.
BONAMY DOBREE. Translated by E. O. LORIMER   *About 21s.*

SOCIOLOGICAL APPROACH TO THE STUDY OF HISTORY

The Aftermath of the Napoleonic Wars: The Concert of Europe—An Experiment
by H. G. SCHENK, D.Phil. (Oxon)   *In preparation. Illustrated. About 21s.*

Progress and Disenchantment: A Comparative Study of European Romanticism
by H. G. SCHENK, D.Phil. (Oxon)   *Illustrated. About 21s.*

SOCIOLOGY OF LAW

The Sociology of Law
by GEORGES GURVITCH, formerly Prof. of Sociology, University of
Strassbourg, France. With an Introduction by ROSCOE POUND, Prof.
of Jurisprudence, late Dean of the Faculty of Law, Harvard University
In preparation. About 21s.

The Institutions of Civil Law and Their Social Functions
by KARL RENNER, Chancellor of the Austrian Republic. Edited with an
Introduction by O. KAHN-FREUND, Ll.M., Dr. Jur., Lecturer in Law,
University of London   *About 10s. 6d.*

Corporations and Their Control
by A. B. LEVY, Dr. Jur., C.L.S., Cantab.   *2 vols.   About 18s. each*

The Control of Industrial Combinations
by ANDREW NEUGROSCHEL, Ph.D., Dr. Jur., Dr. Pol., of the Middle
Temple, Barrister-at-Law   *About 15s.*

Legal Aid
by ROBERT EGERTON, Hon. Sec. Legal Sub-committee Cambridge House, Solicitor of the Supreme Court. With an Introduction by D. L. GOODHART, K.C., D.C.L., Ll.D., Prof. of Jurisprudence, Oxford *10s. 6d.*

Soviet Legal Theory: Its Social Background and Development
by RUDOLF SCHLESINGER, Ph.D., London   *16s.*

CRIMINOLOGY AND THE SOCIAL SERVICES

Criminal Justice and Social Reconstruction
by HERMANN MANNHEIM, Dr. Jur., Lecturer in Criminology in the University of London   *In preparation. About 25s.*

The Psycho-Analytical Approach to Juvenile Delinquency: Theory, Case Studies, Treatment
by KATE FRIEDLANDER, M.D., L.R.C.P. (Edin.), D.P.M. (Lond.), Hon. Psychiatrist, Inst. for the Scientific Treatment of Delinquency; Clinical Dir., W. Sussex Child Guidance Service   *In preparation. About 21s.*

Voluntary Social Services in Britain
by HENRY A. MESS, late Reader in Social Science in the University of London. Edited by GERTRUDE WILLIAMS, Lecturer in Economics, University of London   *About 21s.*

SOCIOLOGY AND POLITICS

The Analysis of Political Behaviour: An Empirical Approach
by HAROLD D. LASSWELL, Formerly Prof. Polit. Science in the University of Chicago, now Director, War Communications Research, Library of Congress   *In preparation. About 18s.*

Democracy, Political Representation and the Electoral System: An Analysis of Fundamentals
by GERHARD LEIBHOLZ, Dr. Phil.   *About 21s.*

Dictatorship and Political Police

The Technique of Control by Fear by E. K. BRAMSTEDT, Ph.D. (London)

15s.

Nationality in History and Politics

by FREDERICK HERTZ, Author of "Race and Civilisation"

Second Impression. 25s.

The American Dilemma

The Negro Problem and Modern Democracy by GUNNAR MYRDAL, Prof. of Political Economy and Public Finance, Stockholm Univ.

2 vols. About £2. 2s.

FOREIGN AFFAIRS, THEIR SOCIAL, POLITICAL AND ECONOMIC FOUNDATIONS

Patterns of Peacemaking

by DAVID THOMSON, Ph.D., Cantab., Research Fellow of Sidney Sussex Coll., Cambridge; E. MEYER, Dr. rer. pol., and A. BRIGGS, B.A., Cantab.

21s.

French Canada in Transition

by EVERETT C. HUGHES, Professor of Sociology, University of Chicago

In preparation. About 18s.

State and Economics in the Middle East

by A. BONNE, Dr. œc. publ., Director, Economic Research Institute of Palestine

About 25s.

Economic Development of the Middle East

An Outline of Planned Reconstruction by A. BONNE, Dr. œc. publ., Director, Economic Research Institute of Palestine

Second Impression. 12s. 6d.

Federalism in Central and Eastern Europe

by RUDOLF SCHLESINGER, Ph.D., London

30s.

The Danube Basin and the German Economic Sphere

by ANTONIN BASCH, Dr. Phil., Columbia Univ,

18s.

The Regions of Germany
by R. E. DICKINSON, Reader in Geography, University College, London
Second Impression. 10s. 6d.

MIGRATION AND RE-SETTLEMENT

Economics of Migration
by JULIUS ISAAC, Ph.D., London. With an Introduction by A. M. CARR-
SAUNDERS, Director of the London School of Economics   *About 21s.*

Co-operative Communities at Work: A Comparative Study
by HENRIK INFIELD, Director, Rural Settlement Inst., New York
In preparation. About 15s.

ECONOMIC PLANNING

Plan for Reconstruction
by W. H. HUTT, Prof. of Commerce, University of Capetown
Second Impression. 18s.

Danger Spots in the New Economic Controls
by Dr. F. BURCHARDT and G. D. N. WORSWICK, Institute of
Statistics, University of Oxford   *About 15s.*

Retail Trade Associations
A New Form of Monopolist Organisation in Britain, by HERMANN
LEVY, Author of "The New Industrial System"   *Second Impression. 15s.*

The Shops of Britain: A Study in Retail Trade Distribution
by HERMANN LEVY   *About 21s.*

The Price of Social Security—The Problem of Labour Mobility
by GERTRUDE WILLIAMS, Lecturer in Economics, University of London
Second Impression. 12s. 6d.

The Changing Pattern of Demand
by CHARLES MADGE   *About 15s.*

7

SOCIOLOGY OF THE FAMILY AND ALLIED TOPICS

Nation and Family

The Swedish Experiment in Democratic Family and Population Policy by ALVA MYRDAL *21s.*

The Sociology of Women's Work

by GERTRUDE WILLIAMS, Lecturer in Economics, University of London *About 15s.*

The Adolescent: A Psychological Sociological Approach

by C. M. FLEMING, Ed.B., Ph.D., University of London Institute of Education *About 15s.*

TOWN AND COUNTRY PLANNING. HUMAN ECOLOGY

Creative Demobilisation

Vol. I. Principles of National Planning
By E. A. GUTKIND, D.Ing.

Vol. 2. Case Studies in National Planning
Edited by E. A. GUTKIND, D.Ing. *Second Impression. 21s. each*

Revolution of Environment

by E. A. GUTKIND, D.Ing. *About 30s.*

The Journey to Work

by K. LIEPMANN, Ph.D., London. With an Introduction by A. M. Carr-Saunders, Director of the London School of Economics
Second Impression. 15s.

City, Region and Regionalism

by ROBERT E. DICKINSON, Reader in Geography, University College, London. With Maps and Plans *In preparation. About 25s.*

SOCIOLOGICAL STUDIES OF MODERN COMMUNITIES

The Anthropology of some Coloured Communities in Great Britain with Comparative Material on Colour Prejudice

by E. K LITTLE, Ph.D., London *In preparation. About 15s.*

Co-operative Living in Palestine
by HENRIK F. INFIELD, Director, Rural Settlement Inst., New York
In preparation. Illustrated. 7s. 6d.

ANTHROPOLOGY AND COLONIAL POLICY

Malay Fishermen: Their Peasant Economy
by RAYMOND FIRTH, Prof. of Anthropology, University of London
Illustrated. 25s. net

The Malay Peasant
An Economic Survey of Past Conditions and Future Problems by
RAYMOND FIRTH, Prof. of Anthropology, University of London
About 21s.

Peasant Life in China
by HSIAO T'UNG FEI, Ph.D., London *Third Impression. Illustrated. 15s.*

Hsinlung Hsiang
A Field Study of Peasant Life in the Red Basin, West China
by ISABEL CROOK and YU HSI-CHI *About 21s.*

A Japanese Village: Suye Mura
by JOHN P. EMBREE, Visiting Assoc. Prof. of Anthropology, University
of Chicago. With an Introduction by A. R. RADCLIFFE-BROWN,
Professor of Social Anthropology, Oxford University
In preparation. Illustrated. 18s.

The Golden Wing: A Family Chronicle
by LIN HUEH-HWA, with an Introduction by BRUNO LASKER,
Internat. Secretariat, Inst. of Pacific Relations *About 15s.*

SOCIOLOGY AND PSYCHOLOGY OF THE PRESENT CRISIS

Diagnosis of Our Time
by KARL MANNHEIM, Lecturer in Sociology, University of London
Third Impression. 10s. 6d.

Farewell to European History—Beyond Nihilism
by ALFRED WEBER *About 30s.*

9

The Fear of Freedom
by Dr. ERICH FROMM   *Third Impression.* *15s.*

Human Nature and Enduring Peace
Edited by GARDNER MURPHY, Professor, The College of the City of New York   *About 15s.*

The Autonomy of Science
by MICHAEL POLANYI, F.R.S., Prof. of Chemistry, University of Manchester   *About 15s.*

SOCIAL PSYCHOLOGY AND PSYCHO-ANALYSIS

Psychology and the Social Pattern
by JULIAN BLACKBURN, Ph.D., B.Sc. (Econ.), Lecturer on Social Psychology, London School of Economics   *Second Impression.* *10s. 6d.*

The Framework of Human Behaviour
by JULIAN BLACKBURN, Ph.D., B.Sc. (Econ.), Lecturer on Social Psychology, London School of Economics   *About 10s. 6d.*

Individual Development in Society
by JULIAN BLACKBURN, Ph.D., B.Sc. (Econ.), Lecturer on Social Psychology, London School of Economics   *About 10s. 6d.*
(Three independent volumes supplementing each other)

A Handbook of Social Psychology
by KIMBALL YOUNG, Professor of Sociology, Queens College, New York   *21s.*

Freud—An Introduction
Selected Readings and a Study concerning the Relationship between Psycho-analysis and Sociology by WALTER HOLLITSCHER, Dr. Phil.
About 15s.

Social Learning and Imitation
by NEAL E. MILLER and JOHN DOLLARD of the Institute of Human Relations, Yale University   *15s.*

Frustration and Aggression
by JOHN DOLLARD, LEONARD E. DOOB, NEAL E. MILLER, O. H. MOWRER, ROBERT R. SEARS, etc., of the Institute of Human Relations, Yale University   *10s. 6d.*

APPROACHES TO THE PROBLEM
OF PERSONALITY

The Cultural Background of Personality
by RALPH LINTON, Professor of Anthropology, Columbia University

About 12s. 6d.

The Feminine Character. The History of an Ideology
by VIOLA KLEIN, Ph.D., London. With an Introduction by KARL MANNHEIM, Dr. Phil., Lecturer in Sociology, University of London

12s. 6d.

The History of Autobiography in Antiquity
by GEORG MISCH. Translated by E. W. DICKES   *About 21s.*

PHILOSOPHICAL AND SOCIAL FOUNDATIONS
OF THOUGHT

The Political Element in Economic Theory
by GUNNAR MYRDAL, Professor of Political Economy and Public Finance, University of Stockholm   *About 21s.*

The Ideal Foundations of Economic Thought
by W. STARK, Dr. rer. pol., Dr. Jur.   *Second Impression. 15s.*

The History of Economics in Its Relation to Social Development
by W. STARK, Dr. rer. pol., Dr. Jur.   *Second Impression. 7s. 6d.*

The Decline of Liberalism as an Ideology
by J. H. HALLOWELL   *In preparation. About 10s. 6d.*

Society and Nature: A Sociological Inquiry
by HANS KELSEN, Formerly Prof. of Law, Vienna and Geneva, Department of Political Science, University of California *In preparation. About 21s.*

GENERAL SOCIOLOGY

A Handbook of Sociology
by W. F. OGBURN, Professor of Sociology, University of Chicago, and M. F. NIMKOFF, Professor of Sociology, Bucknell University

In preparation. About 30s.

11

FOREIGN CLASSICS OF SOCIOLOGY

Wilhelm Dilthey: Selected Readings from his Works and an Introduction to his Sociological and Philosophical Work

by H. A. HODGES, Prof. of Philosophy, University of Reading   *10s. 6d.*

George Herbert Mead: An Introduction

Selected Readings from his Works with an Introduction to his Sociological and Philosophical Writings by Dr. MILTON B. SINGER, University of Chicago   *About 21s.*

Science, Politics and Power

Selected Essays, translated from the Works of MAX WEBER, with an Introduction   *About 15s.*

DOCUMENTARY

Peace Aims of the United Nations

Documents and Readings. Edited by DAVID THOMSON, Ph.D., Cantab, Research Fellow of Sidney Sussex College, Cambridge, and E. MEYER, Dr. rer. pol.   *About 21s.*

Changing Attitudes in Soviet Russia

Documents and Readings concerning the *Family*
Edited by R. SCHLESINGER, Ph.D., London   *About 21s.*

Changing Attitudes in Soviet Russia

Documents and Readings concerning *National Autonomy and Experiments in Administrative Devolution*
Edited by R. SCHLESINGER, Ph.D., London   *About 21s.*

Changing Attitudes in Soviet Russia

Documents and Readings concerning *Foreign Policy*
Edited by R. SCHLESINGER, Ph.D., London   *About 21s.*

All prices are net

Publishers in the United States of America
OXFORD UNIVERSITY PRESS, NEW YORK

THE WESTMINSTER PRESS, LONDON, W.9

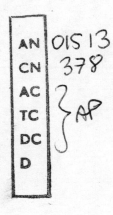